Duty of Care

PTSD, Psychological Injury
Occupational stress & mental
Health in Policing

Claire McDowall

Copyright © 2014 Claire McDowall

All rights reserved.

ISBN:1497372968
ISBN-13:978-1497372962

DEDICATION

This book is for my husband, Police Officer of 19 years and PTSD sufferer and for all Police Officers affected by the issues raised in this book.

CONTENTS

	Introduction	1
	Development of this book	5
1	**Understanding Psychological Injury**	9
	Signs and symptoms of Post-Traumatic Stress……...	9
	Why am I experiencing Post-Traumatic Stress?..........	14
	What are Flashbacks and intrusive memories?..............	27
	Hallucinations……………………………………..	28
2	**Police Culture**	31
	Leadership and Management………………………...	43
	The organization as a potential perpetrator of abuse………………………………………………	46
	Enabling factors……………………………………	47
	Character, Temperament and the Police personality………………………………………..	50
3	**Conclusions on Police Culture**	55
	Badge of honour…………………………………..	61
4	**How many Officers are affected**	63
5	**Good Practice guide for Constabularies**	69
	Comradery……………………………………...........	74
	Critical Incident Debrief & Mandatory counselling….	75
	Supervisions…………………………………………	76
	Working to policy (Welfare)…………………………	78
	Health and Safety Executive Management Standards..	79
	Transparency and integrity & clear communication…	80
	Challenging the culture of bullying and intimidation...	81
	Health and Wellbeing surveys………………………..	82
	Person centered support……………………………..	82

	Re-Victimization (traumatization) of the Officer......	84
	Distortion, Deletion and Generalization.................	87
	Distrust and deception....................................	91
	Good Practice Guidance for Occupational Health Advisors..	93
	Understanding the Onset of PTSD......................	99
	Good practice guidance for HR........................	101
	Golden rules for organizations...........................	101
6	**Advocacy with your employer**	**105**
	Personal journal..	107
	Communications...	108
	Tackling organizational deviancy with logic and rationale...	109
	Know your policies and procedures.....................	110
	Grievance...	111
	Legal representation......................................	112
	Discrimination claim.....................................	113
	Employment Tribunal – Useful facts....................	113
	Workplace Injury..	114
	Injury on Duty Award.....................................	114
	Annual leave during long term sickness absence........	115
	Appeal against reduction to pay.........................	116
	Getting your employer to understand your circumstances...	117
	HR and Occupational Health records...................	119
	Accountability..	119
	Request a sickness review meeting......................	120
	Force Medical Advisor appointment....................	123
	Contracted psychologist..................................	124
	Recording meetings.......................................	124
	Early Ill Health Retirement (EIHR).....................	125
	Deviant behaviour in the organization..................	127

7	**Living with Psychological Injury**	129
	Coping strategies and Safety strategies	129
	What does PTS say about me?	130
	Measuring PTSD	131
	Police Trauma Spectrum	132
	Risks associated with Post-Traumatic Stress	133
	Potential impact on family life and relationships	134
	Self-actualization	134
	Lifestyle choice	136
	Social integration	138
	Disclosure	139
	How can family and friends help?	140
	Animal therapy	142
	Self-assessment of Risk and Safety Plan	143
	Self-harm or suicide	145
	On the edge of life and death	146
	Criminal offence	147
	Risk Safety Plan	148
	A note on Disability	151
8	**Carers and Family**	157
	The risk of suicide	160
	Talking to children about PTS	161
	Domestic Violence and abuse in the context of PTSD	164
9	**Support, Advice & Financial Help**	167
10	**Conclusion & Recommendations**	171
	Appendices	179
	Bibliography	193
	Useful Links	202
	About the Author	205
	Index	207

Claire McDowall

INTRODUCTION

Our family was affected by my husband's stress breakdown and he was diagnosed with complex PTSD (post-traumatic stress disorder). The experience was life changing and we felt uncertainty, fear, anxiety and isolation.

My husband approached Occupational Health with Work related stress on three separate occasions over the course of 8 years. No screening for Psychological injury or stress assessment was completed and the only support offered was external counselling sessions (not appropriate treatment for PTSD). There were no adjustments made to reduce his stress in the workplace and no one monitored or reviewed his wellbeing.

He finally collapsed after living with undiagnosed Post-Traumatic Stress (PTS) for over thirteen years, serving as a Police Officer. An incident involving line managers resulted in a stress overload. Although he had experienced bullying and intimidation throughout his career; it was the single act of his line managers coming to his home address and persistently pounding on his front door when he was off sick, that he felt was in breach of trust, integrity and courtesy. It was the manner in which they behaved which caused him distress. He perceived it to be disrespectful to his family and a breach of his only sanctuary and safe haven. It felt to him that they had broken down his last remaining wall of protection and there was a strong feeling of violation.

We were then thrown into a confusing and frightening period of adjustment with home life and work. We became aware through contact with the mental health team that it is common place for Police Officers to be affected by post-traumatic stress. We also know there is a culture within the Police service making it difficult to open up and discuss psychological injury and mental ill health.

Families need support too, finding ways to cope, keep well and care for their loved one. Families can be significantly affected.

In his nineteen years serving as a Police Officer; my husband was unaware of support available via his employer, such as critical incident debrief and mandatory counselling. His belief was that Post-Traumatic Stress was a disorder reserved for the armed forces (combat stress). Now in hindsight he can recall many Officers he has worked with who have demonstrated signs of trauma. The Psychologist contracted by the force explained to him that he had seen over 300 Officers in the last two years in his force area alone.

Research into PTSD, 'Moral Injury', 'Police Culture' and Community Policing, come together in this book to highlight concerns over the psychological health of Police Officers; drawing on early research in the 1960's through to 2013.

This book is designed to be informative and supportive with practical advice on living with PTS, assisting Police Officers, their partners and family, encouraging change in attitudes towards Psychological injury and mental health in the Police service, improve support provision, encourage early detection and risk assessment and overcome isolation.

Duty of Care

This book provides information and advice around what you should expect from your employer and offers guidance to organisations on best practice.

Our personal experiences including pitfalls and possible solutions, ways we learned to live alongside PTS (a work in progress!) and employer/employee relationship are discussed. This book is intended to be a support handbook and is no substitution for professional help and advice. If you are affected by any of the issues raised in this book you are advised to see your G.P who can refer you to appropriate agencies and services and provide you with support. It is hoped that Constabularies will use the information herein as a learning opportunity and adopt practices which protect them from litigation and enable an efficient and committed workforce.

Although the main focus of this book is on PTS, there is a wealth of advice and information which will be of use to Police Officers with mental ill health and workplace stress. Knowing the signs and symptoms of PTS means the ability to self-identify this condition at an early stage. Identities have been protected throughout the book. A real case study (Robert) has been used to demonstrate difficulties faced by many Officers.

Take care when reading this book and take your time. I have not included details of trauma. There will most likely be frustrations and difficulties mentioned here which strike a chord with you and your own experience. This can increase your anger levels. Think about safety measures you would like to put in place when reading. Think about the time of day you choose to read (certainly not before bed!). Do you need someone to talk to afterwards?

DEVELOPMENT OF THIS BOOK

This book began with the intention of creating a brief information booklet on PTSD for Police Officers. It was hoped that it would empower them to understand their symptoms regardless of whether or not they had a diagnosis, or had acknowledged symptoms of occupational stress and trauma.

Our experience of the Constabulary as employer with a duty of care, a protracted and unsupportive period of sickness absence, badly managed grievance, disability discrimination and subsequent legal action was an education for me as an 'outsider'. Internal systems, attitudes, management of Constables, how the organization deals with complainants, mental ill health, long term sickness absence, disability, welfare, occupational health and Personnel support are culturally very different from other work sectors. The book grew as a result, to include a broader picture of 'the Constabulary' as an institution, what to expect as an employee, employment rights and advocacy.

The motivation for the book came from a desire to prevent (as far as possible), the extreme of complex PTSD, relationship difficulties and isolation for others, which we ourselves had to painfully negotiate. The book draws on two years of personal experience of communication and involvement with the organization during long term sickness absence and beyond; ultimately resulting in legal action. During this time we were also learning to come to terms with a new way of life and my husbands' disability.

The drive to understand PTS and associated symptoms and behaviour has informed this book. We discovered the work of Dr. Jonathan Shay quite by accident when my husband theorized the relationship between Berserkers and his feelings about PTSD.

Dr. Shay is our hero. When all other information on PTSD fell short, his books (Achilles in Vietnam and Odysseus in America) invoked the exclamation 'Eureka'; particularly in relation to 'Moral Injury'. His direction to the work of Judith Herman M.D (Trauma and Recovery) provided further validation.

After writing about our experiences, I realized that without evidence to support my work, the book would account for little more than a personal belief. I needed to demonstrate authenticity to those able to take my ideas and utilize them in organizational reform. Research was also important for highlighting that personal examples in the book are not as 'far-fetched' as they would seem to an outsider of the force. Therefore, I began looking for research to reinforce the messages in the book or dispute them.

The first paper I found was by Heather Coombe, 'To what extent does Police occupational culture impact on social and domestic lives of Police Officers?', Plymouth Law and Criminal Justice Review 2013. I was immediately struck by the reference she made to behaviour found in Police culture which epitomized behaviour I had already come to associate with Post-trauma symptoms (such as alcoholism, emotional detachment, cynicism, suspicion, danger and altered cognitive behaviour). Following her references I discovered a plethora of research on Police culture which opened up further discussion in this book on other influences on PTS.

Information was sourced via Home Office and HSE (Health and Safety Executive) publications. What I believed to be a topic which is under-researched by government bodies turned out to be a subject which received some attention years ago. Unfortunately and frustratingly it seems that knowledge and information on PTS or Psychological injury; though communicated to government officials and bodies such as ACPO; have failed to be communicated to all ranks of Officer. Information on good practice for the organization has been included in policies and procedures and yet this information is not being utilized, followed or acted upon. In light of this; I hope the book will bridge the gap between knowledge held by the upper echelons and front line Officers, because knowledge is power and I wish for my work to empower you to confidently expect dignity, respect and support from your supervisors and employer. This is particularly important as findings suggest a strong link between the organization and it's practices with higher levels of PTS symptoms and as the main contributing factor to PTS, over and above any impact of a traumatic incident.

For any academics reading this book; I apologize for any negligence relating to this work. This would be unconsciously done as would any inadequate referencing and literary skill. I have tried to limit secondary references. This has not always been possible; due to the financial implications of purchasing an array of journals and books (I have been working as a full-time carer and advocate to my husband and mother of three children, so the purse strings are an issue). I have edited and formatted this work. I hope you can forgive me any shortcomings as I have been self-taught through the process of writing this book. In any event; my main aim has been and always will be, primarily the purpose of supporting Officers, validating their experiences, giving solace and enabling change. Information in this edition is correct at the point of publication in 2014.

1 UNDERSTANDING PSYCHOLOGICAL INJURY

Signs and symptoms of Post-Traumatic Stress

I have decided to begin the book with signs and symptoms. Should the first few pages be the only opportunity I have to get important information to you (should you tire and lose interest too soon); I want you to know what to look out for and give yourself a health check and seek help early.

Take a look at the possible symptoms listed here. If you notice signs of occupational stress or Post-Traumatic Stress (PTS) seek help early through your GP, your Occupational Health Department and social networks (including family). Be prepared for the fact that you may experience most or all of the items listed.

One of the first steps is to identify the likelihood an Officer is experiencing PTS. Ideally; line managers, occupational health and welfare workers should explore symptoms of PTS with Officers who present with stress related behaviours. This is an area in need of much improvement.

Partners are likely to notice changes in behaviour and may attribute these behaviours to dissatisfaction in the relationship. Partners can be empowered to help and understand what is happening within their relationship through raising awareness of signs and symptoms.

The individual can take responsibility for self-identifying PTS when they are given information, validation, and support and (in some cases) permission to acknowledge PTS rather than deny their experiences.

The American Psychiatric Association (APA) reviewed the criteria for PTSD in 2013 and have published DSM-5[1] (Diagnostic and Statistical Manual of Mental Disorders), consisting of eight criteria (A-H).

Criteria A relates to a 'stressor' such as exposure to death, threatened death, actual or threatened serious injury or actual or threatened sexual violence in at least one of the following ways:-
1)Direct exposure to
2)Witnessing in person
3)Indirectly and relating to a close friend or family member
4)Repeated or extreme indirect exposure to aversive details of the event(s) (usually in the course of professional duties, e.g. first responders and repeated exposure to details of abuse)

It is not necessary for Flashbacks to be present for the individual to meet the criteria of PTSD. Criteria B sets out symptoms of 'intrusion' which can be involuntary memories, flashbacks, nightmares, intense and prolonged distress after exposure to traumatic reminders or significant physiological reactions to trauma-related stimulus. Only one of these need apply. Police Officers are persistently

---

[1] (DSM-5 Criteria for PTSD, 2013)

exposed to 'Stressors' and trauma related stimuli during the course of their 'normal policing duties'. Studies have shown[2] that Police Officers can be affected by partial or subsyndromal PTSD where symptoms have not met the full diagnostic criteria and therefore the individual can be significantly affected by Post-Traumatic Stress. It is important to note that other conditions may be present alongside PTS, such as Generalized Anxiety or Depression. Compassion Fatigue, Burnout, Vicarious Traumatization and Secondary Traumatic Stress may also be part of the Police Officers' experience[3] and this is discussed later in the book. The individual will likely experience many of the following symptoms and behaviours:-

Physical symptoms of Post-Traumatic Stress may include:-
- ❖ Frequent headaches/migraine
- ❖ Muscle aches
- ❖ Lethargy/persistent tiredness or feelings of exhaustion
- ❖ Onset of Asthma
- ❖ Chest pain/tightness in the chest
- ❖ Spasms/flinching or startling
- ❖ Frequent stomach cramps
- ❖ Excessive sleep or difficulty sleeping/ irregular sleep patterns
- ❖ Loss of libido

---

[2] (Maguen, Metzier, Inslicht, Henn-Haase, Neylan, & Marmar, 2009), (Carlier, Lamberts, & Gersons, 1997), (Marmar & McCaslin, 2006)

[3] (Salston & Figley, 2003)

Emotional symptoms of Post-Traumatic Stress may include:-
- ❖ Tearfulness
- ❖ Persistent feelings of anger
- ❖ Rage/outbursts of anger disproportionate to the situation
- ❖ Feelings of intense hatred for someone
- ❖ Feelings of anxiety, guilt, shame
- ❖ Feeling you pose a real risk of harm to others
- ❖ Feeling there is no escape from the situation
- ❖ Feeling empty or numb

Psychological symptoms of Post-Traumatic Stress may include:-
- ❖ Flashbacks, intrusive memories
- ❖ Nightmares
- ❖ Some degree of depression
- ❖ Thoughts of suicide
- ❖ Planning suicide
- ❖ Worries about mental ill health
- ❖ Worries about how others will see you, stigma around mental ill health and perceiving the self to be weak
- ❖ Hyper-vigilance and alertness on and off duty
- ❖ Constant scanning for threats on or off duty
- ❖ Forgetfulness
- ❖ Confusion
- ❖ Distrust of others
- ❖ Overwhelming despair

Behaviour associated with Post-Traumatic Stress may include:-
- ❖ Frequent use of pain relief
- ❖ Withdrawal from family and friends
- ❖ Disinterestedness

Duty of Care

- ❖ Desire to be alone
- ❖ Difficulty with social interactions
- ❖ Difficulty with crowds
- ❖ Avoidance of places, people, type of work/duty
- ❖ High and/or frequent alcohol consumption or substance use
- ❖ Scanning and hyper-vigilance on and off duty
- ❖ Rapid Eye Movement during flashbacks
- ❖ Flinching/startling/jumping
- ❖ Rapid escalation in anger or reacting with anger, disproportionate to the situation
- ❖ Explosive anger
- ❖ Agitated body language
- ❖ Hard expression in the face/look of distance
- ❖ Self-incarceration in the home to safeguard others and reduce risk of offending behaviour
- ❖ Difficulty leaving the house without a trusted companion or partner
- ❖ Quickly angered or agitated by the perceived pettiness of others moans, groans and squabbles
- ❖ Impatience
- ❖ Family breakdown/separation from partner
- ❖ Isolation
- ❖ Reluctance to drive or drive distances
- ❖ Repeated checking of home security and car security (for example)
- ❖ Self-harm
- ❖ Self-destructive/reckless behaviour (including alcoholism, sexual promiscuity, seeking out dangerous activity)

Barriers to self-identifying Post-Traumatic Stress may include:-
- Behaviour such as alertness, hyper-vigilance, scanning and concerns over home security are synonymous with the role of a Police Officer
- Culturally speaking it is commonplace for Police Officers to experience family breakdown or separation, infidelity and increase in alcohol consumption.
- Behaviour is likely to creep in over time
- Many physical symptoms are mistaken for flu or viral infection
- Intrusive symptoms can, in some cases, be viewed as mere 'memories'
- Distrust of others may be attributed to the experience of Policing and dealing with deception and dishonesty
- Police Officers are expected to deal with stressful, traumatic or dangerous events frequently in their role and not be affected.
- Coping or safety strategies may be developed over time, become habitual and therefore normal for the individual.
- Individuals may not want to acknowledge difficulties with mental ill health
- 'Police Personality' is identified as cynical, emotionally detached, suspicious etc. and therefore seen as a normal part of 'Police Culture' rather than potential symptoms.

Why am I experiencing Post-Traumatic Stress?

Police Officers are exposed to events which, for most of us are not part of normal everyday life. This is particularly true of the frequency and volume of events. People may be affected by trauma at some point in their life and have time to come to terms with this event and continue to view their

Duty of Care

environment and others as generally safe and secure. Police Officers may find they view the world as generally unsafe, dishonest and threatening. This world view is a result of exposure to victim trauma as well as ones' own experiences. Challenging the individuals' belief system around safety and security results in VT (Vicarious Traumatization)[4]

Some examples of potentially traumatic events on duty are:[5]
- ❖ Sudden deaths
- ❖ Unexplained deaths
- ❖ Mutilated body/body parts/decomposed body
- ❖ Presence at scene of death of child
- ❖ Working with cases of child abuse/investigating indecent child images
- ❖ Road Traffic Collision, particularly involving fatality or serious injury
- ❖ Threat to life on duty, including threat with a weapon
- ❖ Any event involving serious physical injury to self or colleagues
- ❖ Death of colleague on duty
- ❖ Major incidents involving many casualties
- ❖ Firearm incident

"Professionals…who work with crime victims deserve a lot of credit." (Salston & Figley, 2003) Front line Officers are exposed to regular second hand trauma (Secondary Traumatic Stress) from taking statements, investigating violent crime and abuse, supporting victims and delivering death messages to families. The role of the Officer may result in STS (Secondary Traumatic Stress), Compassion Fatigue or Countertransference[6].

---

[4] (Salston & Figley, 2003)

[5] (Critical Incident Debrief 'cldB' Force Policy, 2004)

[6] (Salston & Figley, 2003)

"trauma is contagious" (Herman, 1997:140), *"Repeated exposure to stories of human rapacity and cruelty inevitably challenges the [individuals'] basic faith... [and] heightens [their] sense of personal vulnerability"* (Herman, 1997: 141).

In addition to first hand trauma experienced by the Officer; STS contributes to the individuals' belief that the world is unsafe.[7] PTS symptoms can be experienced as a result of STS and Compassion Fatigue. The APA (American Psychological Association) recognizes the parallels between full diagnostic PTSD and Compassion Fatigue. Though the individual with Compassion Fatigue did not share in the victims' traumatic experience directly; they can still be affected by their trauma, including nightmares about the event.[8]

The Officer is susceptible to Compassion Fatigue when s/he genuinely sympathizes with the victim and works with a desire to aid the person who is suffering. S/he is likely to have an idealistic belief about how they can help victims rather than recognising their personal limitations. Officers can become affected to the degree that they experience intrusive memories about the victims' trauma and reminders of their case can trigger physiological and behavioural reactions, such as avoidance and hyper-arousal.[9]

It is expected that Police Officers will be exposed to trauma and that they will be affected or distressed by case details and investigations. Support and education which enables Officers to recognise the effects on physical and psychological health and what the individual can do in the interests of early intervention can reduce the impact[10].

---

[7] (Salston & Figley, 2003)
[8] (Salston & Figley, 2003)
[9] (Salston & Figley, 2003)
[10] (Salston & Figley, 2003)

Officers frequently suffer verbal abuse (including threats to them and their family) and aggression. They may be subjected to workplace bullying and intimidation (including fears around job security within a ranking organisation). They may lack support from colleagues and supervisors and can be affected by poor management decisions and poor leadership. This contributes to occupational stress, isolation and feeling unsafe and threatened. A recent survey of 250 Officers in the Metropolitan police highlighted *"bullying culture, threats of misconduct for failing to achieve targets and a workforce at 'rock bottom'"(BBC News)* [11]

Police Officers are faced with aggression, violence and disrespect and are expected to exercise restraint on their emotions and reactions. They are expected to have control over themselves and their behaviour at all times[12]. Adrenaline surges round the body preparing for fight or flight. The Officer can only use necessary and proportionate force[13]. It is a bit like shaking a bottle of fizzy pop and not taking off the lid to let that energy out; keeping a lid on it for years or decades.

Police Officers are (to a large extent) denied their individuality by the public[14], the organization and the Police regulations. One colleague told Robert 'you know we are just a number'. Police Officers are not expected to have an opinion and where it is in conflict with a supervisor it can be viewed as insubordination and the Officer may find themselves bullied and intimidated for speaking up; even if this behaviour is subtle.

There are tensions in a reformed, multicultural and diverse workforce contributing to occupational stress[15].

---

[11] (Met Police Has 'Culture Of Fear', Officers Say, 2014)
[12] (Coombe, 2013)
[13] Code of Ethics – 4 Use of Force
[14] (Loftus, 2012)
[15] (Loftus, 2012)

These factors are on top of normal everyday ups and downs, bereavement or traumatic events in one's personal life[16]. Many Police Officers have long service and this can be up to 30 years. When you add it all up, you realise no-one can accuse the Officer of weakness. Police Officers can feel they have reached saturation point and there may be an event which becomes the catalyst for a stress breakdown. When the Police Officer experiences persistent stress from all angles; it can result in feeling trapped with no escape from the stress. The stress breakdown is followed by a period of vulnerability. For some individuals there is a risk of taking their own life.

Multiple psychological injuries can occur throughout the Officer's career which can stack up; inhibiting psychological recovery after each traumatic event. It is generally believed to be a specific traumatic event which causes PTS. In our experience (and as you will discover through reading this book) it is more likely to be multiple traumatic events, combined with occupational stress, workplace culture and 'Moral Injury' which leads to full diagnostic PTSD.

"When a critical incident is placed within the context of other dissatisfactions within the workplace, this more demanding aspect of police work can be overwhelming" (Mitchell, Stevenson, & Poole, 2001)

"Work environment factors such as dissatisfaction with organizational support predicted PTSD symptoms in police officers" (Carlier et al., 1997)[17]

---

[16] (Maguen, Metzier, Inslicht, Henn-Haase, Neylan, & Marmar, 2009)

[17] (Carlier, Lamberts, & Gersons, 1997: cited in Maguen et al, 2009)

"routine work stressors were associated with PTSD symptoms, and [the] effects were independent from and larger than [those] of cumulative critical incident exposure"(Liberman et al., 2002)[18]

Dr Shay introduced us to what he has identified as 'Moral Injury' involved in trauma. He describes this as a betrayal of 'what's right' by leaders. He believes it is responsible for lifelong psychological injury.[19] He says *"Veterans can usually recover from horror, fear and grief……so long as "what's right" has not been violated"*(Shay, 2003:20).

Complex PTSD (which affects Robert), is where social trust is destroyed due to *"persistent human betrayal and rupture of community in mortal-stakes situations of captivity (even when it has been entered voluntarily)"*(Shay, 2002:160) Police Officers are captives (albeit voluntary), exposed to persistent human betrayal, breakdown of community and at times subjected to abuse of power and authority. This is discussed further throughout the book.

PTS in Policing differs from trauma experienced by the general population. One of the important factors for recovery is the attitude of the Officers' community and how s/he is viewed in that community. For example; putting oneself at risk for a community which largely de-values the individual and shows no gratitude has an impact on the Officer[20] and can result in 'Burnout'[21].

Cultural attitudes within the Police around discussing emotional stress, the impact of upsetting cases and the often brief interval between difficult work events, will likely contribute to impeding recovery from trauma. A period of

---

[18] (Liberman et al., 2002: cited in Maguen, Metzier, Inslicht, Henn-Haase, Neylan, & Marmar, 2009)

[19] (Shay, Achilles In Vietnam: Combat Trauma And The Undoing Of Character, 2003)

[20] (Graef, 1990)

[21] (Karpman, 1984)

'processing' the event, making sense of it and reconciling with it are important for psychological health and wellbeing. Hurriedly pushing thoughts and feelings away following an incident, not allowing one-self to re-assess or evaluate the experience and order those thoughts and feelings is a factor affecting the likelihood of PTS; as does lack of comradery, feeling safe to talk to colleagues in confidence and ability to express oneself without fear. Mechanisms for letting off steam and relieving some of the stress, has largely been removed from within the culture of the Police service.

If you have experienced trauma in your personal life (including bereavement) this can affect your susceptibility to PTS or exacerbate symptoms. Family history of mental ill health and experiences during the formative years (such as abuse) may also be contributing factors.

"In police academy recruits, childhood trauma appears to be a risk factor for the development of subsequent anxiety disorder symptoms"(Otte et al., 2005) [22].

The advice for people affected by PTS as a result of a single trauma (and in a document produced by the federation[23]) is to get back to 'normal' patterns and routines, including a return to work as soon as possible. However; Police Officers are most likely to return to work and be faced with further traumatic events and therefore professional advice and support must be sought in relation to mental wellbeing and the prevention of further psychological trauma on duty. There needs to be recognition within the police service that PTS in Officers is less likely to be as simple as resulting from a single trauma.[24]

---

[22] (Otte et al., 2005: cited in Maguen, Metzier, Inslicht, Henn-Haase, Neylan, & Marmar, 2009)

[23] (Federation, 2009)

[24] (Mitchell, Stevenson, & Poole, 2001)

We can develop Post-Traumatic Stress (PTS) and continue to function 'normally' on a day to day basis. For example getting up, washed and dressed, going to work, going shopping and socialising etc. The individual may adjust to the PTS by (perhaps unknowingly) adopting some coping strategies for dealing with the stress and managing the effects. Subsyndromal PTSD' means post-traumatic symptoms are present and not to the extent that they meet full diagnostic criteria.[25][26] PTS can become a Disability when the individual's normal day to day functioning is significantly affected. For example; the length of time it takes to complete a task, memory loss, confusion and difficulty with socialization etc. For diagnosis PTSD must meet the full diagnostic criteria (currently DSM-5, Diagnostic and Statistical Manual of Mental Disorders)[27]. Symptoms can be mild to severe.

In the passage on 'Why am I experiencing Post-Traumatic Stress' I introduced 'Moral Injury' and the work of Dr. Shay with Vietnam Veterans affected by Psychological injury. Dr. Shay believes people can recover from horrors when there has been no 'Moral Injury' or betrayal of trust and the leaders do 'what's right'.[28] This is especially important in a high stakes situation.

He says poor leadership and Moral Injury in the war zone could result in 'fragging'.[29]

---

[25] (Maguen, Metzier, Inslicht, Henn-Haase, Neylan, & Marmar, 2009)

[26] (Lansing, 2012)

[27] (DSM-5 Criteria for PTSD, 2013)

[28] (Shay, Achilles In Vietnam: Combat Trauma And The Undoing Of Character, 2003)

[29] (Shay, Achilles In Vietnam: Combat Trauma And The Undoing Of Character, 2003)

For example; commanders were assassinated by the men using grenades during combat. In the Police; rebellion against poor leadership is more childish and petulant.

We would do things to irritate; like move things in the gaffer's office, or take his pens instead of going to the stationary cupboard. One Bobby told me he wiped his cock round the rim of the gaffer's mug – (Robert)

Individuals with PTSD have a strong sense of wanting justice for offences against them. People have suggested this is because they want financial compensation. However; Moral Injury sheds light on the individual's motivation for seeking justice. It is an essential part of aiding recovery.

I asked for the sergeant to be spoken to by his line manager, the impact on me explained to him and discuss how he could deal with a situation like this differently in future. An apology would have been nice and some sense that us Bobbies are looked after and protected from bad management choices. Instead they did a cover up and my grievance kept going all the way up to the ACC, and 12 months was spent on this process – (Robert)

Depending on the circumstances; it may be necessary for the individual to have a wider acknowledgment of the wrong-doing, perhaps 'naming and shaming' or public apology etc.

Very often; listening to the Officer's concerns and the impact on him or her[30], discussing how the situation could have been handled differently, a sincere apology for what has occurred and an action plan for doing things differently in future (including using it as a learning opportunity) and communicating this to the Officer, may be sufficient.

---

[30] (Code of Ethics, 2014)

This approach is more cost effective, reduces time and energy dealing with protracted disputes, reduces levels of sickness absence, may reduce the impact of PTS and demonstrates leadership maturity.

More serious cases involving breach of standards of professional behaviour and misconduct must see the offender held accountable and dealt with in accordance with policy and legislation, regardless of rank[31]. Minimising the offence or its consequences will not afford justice to the injured party.

So what can Constabularies learn from the concept of Moral Injury and the role it plays in PTS? What Dr. Shay tells us about Moral Injury is good news for Constabularies across the UK. It means there is much which can be done to reduce the impact of PTS in Officers, aid a more successful recovery and reduce the risk of PTS becoming a lifelong psychological injury.

I was told 'you won't get an apology... you know it' The Welfare officer told me – 'They won't say sorry, are you aware you're making the situation worse by putting in a complaint?, senior officers think they can do what they want, if you move it will resolve the situation, you'll never win, they'll concoct an excuse for what they did'- (Robert)

With changes to workplace culture, the way in which people are promoted through the ranks,[32] ensuring supervisors and the organisation as a whole are held accountable for misconduct,[33] encouraging development of good leadership skills,[34] working to policy and legislation at all levels and treating colleagues with dignity and respect are practical

---

[31] (Code of Ethics, 2014)
[32] (Metcalfe & Dick, 2000)
[33] (Code of Ethics, 2014)
[34] (Metcalfe & Dick, 2000) (Dobby, Anscombe, & Tuffin, 2004) (Mitchell, Stevenson, & Poole, 2001)

solutions to reducing the impact of occupational stress in Officers and are achievable, realistic and cost effective. Even better is the fact systems for achieving this are already in place and only need be enforced.

I have introduced you to 'symptoms' because this is perhaps the easiest starting point for identifying PTS. PTSD is known as a mental illness, a disorder and therefore a condition. There are strong arguments for Post-Traumatic Stress not to be defined as a Disorder.

The trouble with mental ill health is that people can't see what's wrong with you and when you have 'better' days and present as 'normal' you feel like a fake or that people don't believe you. People can understand physical injury easier. It is more measureable and obvious; as are the adaptations people need or develop – (Robert)

Dr Shay says the individual adapts behaviours which helps him/her to survive in stressful environments (combat).[35] Therefore PTSD is not an illness. The behaviours persist (i.e. they cannot be switched off) and adaptations to behaviour are maladaptive in the context of home life. The behaviour of the individual is normal for that person; within their own set of personal circumstances.

For example; the behaviours I highlight around hyper-vigilance and difficulty with trust are in fact necessary behaviours for a Police Officer. These behaviours increase safety. This also explains emotional numbing, withdrawal, detachment and disinterestedness in relationships with friends and family.

The Officer may have difficulty switching off these behaviours when off duty because the threat of harm and wrong-doing continue to exist in the environment in which

---

[35] (Shay, Odysseus In America: Combat Trauma And The Trials Of Homecoming, 2002) (Shay, Achilles In Vietnam: Combat Trauma And The Undoing Of Character, 2003)

they live and work[36] and they are never really 'off duty' because they are always expected to respond to incidents and criminality.[37]

Unfortunately; behaviours associated with PTS are out of context with home life and behaviours can be extreme. Perspective on life and everyday events can become cut and dry. There is a threat or no threat. There is diminished ability to reason that what is perceived as a threat is not a threat in this context. Even a small child at play can trigger a defensive reaction.[38]

Lansing discusses brain activity in those with PTSD, how various affected parts of the brain (responsible for particular behaviours) are over-activated and how evidence of the injury can be seen on SPECT images taken of the brain.[39] The individual with PTS can be affected by persistent feelings of anger and often without knowing what the trigger for the anger is. There can be anxiety that the anger will manifest quickly and without warning, be uncontrollable and explosive. The individual can become exhausted by exerting mammoth efforts to keep a lid on emotions and behaviours; hence symptoms of headache and muscular aches and pains etc.

In our society it is unacceptable to act in ways which are violent and aggressive; either because of social etiquette, morality or legality. For the most part; we are brought up to respect one another, be polite and courteous. There can be a wide disparity between the morals and integrity of the individual compared with the thoughts, feelings and subsequent desire to cause harm to others; either one who has perpetrated or perpetrates harm against the individual or indiscriminate anger, rage or violence against someone in

---

[36] (Mitchell, Stevenson, & Poole, 2001)
[37] (Coombe, 2013)
[38] (Lansing, 2012)
[39] (Lansing, 2012)

the wrong place at the wrong time. The individual of good moral character experiencing violent thoughts and feelings; will likely face the real fear of causing harm and acting in ways which contradict their beliefs, code of conduct and principles. They may have a *"fear of becoming a monster"* (Lansing, 2012:49). There is a strong pull for the individual to withdrawal from people and society and isolate themselves as a means to protect others from their unpredictable behaviour. Lansing refers to this as 'the call of the man cave'. She highlights this as the most dangerous consequence of PTSD, because isolation and loneliness means it is easier to lose hope and we are creatures who need 'the herd'.[40] Isolation is therefore life threatening. Behaviours associated with PTS are out of sync with the expectations of and polite rules of engagement with society. There is likely to be thoughts and feelings of wanting revenge and seeking justice through violence. The individual may have hallucinations about acts of violence against their perpetrator, which are graphic, gruesome and pleasurable.[41] They may plan out (to some degree) where and when the revenge will take place and how they will gain access to the perpetrator.

Summary

So perhaps the psychological and behavioural traits in the individual are not an illness, but normal for that individual in their circumstances. PTSD is an injury to the brain which can be seen with imaging equipment. The physiological symptoms are mostly the result of hyper-arousal (fight, flight or avoidance) and suppressing behaviours which are not acceptable in the wider community or congruent with the morals and ethics of the individual.

---

[40] (Lansing, 2012)
[41] (Herman, 1997)

Behaviour which is normal or has become normal for the individual is viewed as abnormal within society as a whole. For the PTS sufferer; the fight or flight response may be overpowering rational thoughts. The individual can react to any perceived threat without evaluating the situation. For example; regardless of the size, age or gender of the person who is the threat. Very often there is only 'threat' or 'no threat'. Analysis of the situation, consequences of actions or what the consequences could have been if acted upon; may not be visited until later. The individual is wired for survival.

PTS symptoms are most likely due to first hand trauma, STS, VT, Compassion Fatigue and organizational considerations.

What are Flashbacks and intrusive memories?

When I woke in the night; the scene where she was hanging in the shower was superimposed in my bedroom. It was so real. She was real – (Robert)

Flashbacks are the experience of re-living a traumatic event or remembering traumatic events without first calling on these memories; therefore, they are intrusive, unwelcome and uncontrolled. Reliving the traumatic event is experienced as the event happening again.[42] It feels real and can be a three dimensional experience; often including sounds, smells, tastes and physical sensation. People in the flashback can appear as solid and real. There may be a fear of 'getting lost' in the experience and the individual may feel temporarily out of contact with reality.

---

[42] (NICE Guidelines: Post Traumatic Stress Disorder: The management of PTSD in adults and children in primary and secondary care, 2005)

I could be talking to someone and they would never guess I was seeing images rush through my mind at the same time – (Robert)

Intrusive memories can appear without being summoned by the individual. There may be no control mechanism for adjusting the intensity, tuning in or out, hitting the pause button or stopping the flashback.

Flashbacks and intrusive memories can vary in duration and intensity. Intrusive memories can jump from one event to another during an episode. Sometimes the individual can experience a rush of images. Frequency and intensity of flashbacks and intrusive memories can vary from one day to another. This may be affected by external triggers, TV viewing, stress levels, anger levels and stimulants such as caffeine etc.

Hallucinations

Hallucinations may be pleasurable and yet disconcerting. The individual may worry it is a sign of madness and disclosure can be daunting. I refer to this experience as hallucination because like a flashback; this can feel real. It can be visualized as if the scene is actually happening and can involve physical sensation and seeing people appear as solid manifestations.

The hallucination is likely to involve fantasy about revenge against those who have betrayed you, pose a threat to you, abused you or failed to protect you. These fantasies are most likely to be brutally violent, graphic and (to some degree) pleasurable. You may visualize yourself in a 'berserker' state and blind rage during this episode. One Officer in 'Talking Blues' describes his reactions to violent riots. He sought psychiatric help and described a vivid dream of himself murdering people indiscriminately who had been a threat to him during this event.

He recalls it being the most enjoyable dream he has ever had in his life.[43] Where the perpetrator is felt to be the organization; such as resulting from poor leadership and decisions which place the individual in danger or where the organisation mistreats the Officer; there can be a transference of rage from the public offender to the supervisors responsible for the Officer's welfare. Their failure to protect the individual in their capacity as 'care giver' may result in preoccupation with plans for revenge; not against the anti-social offender, but the supervisor or organisation with a duty of care for the employee.[44] Hallucination may be in response to persistent and prolonged abuse, threat, betrayal or trauma, where there is a sense of not being able to escape the situation and powerlessness to stop the abuse of power and authority over the individual. 'Revenge fantasy' gives an outlet for emotions and sees the roles reversed, where the victim becomes the perpetrator and vice versa.[45] Far from being 'mad'; there is a rational reason for the traumatized person to experience 'revenge fantasy' and it is common amongst this group of people.

It was an innocent object I held in my hand. I was talking with my wife about events which made me angry. I entered a hallucination where my abuser was stood in front of me. The innocent object had become a knife in my mind and I visualized myself stabbing him over and over. There was a sensation of blood running over my hands. It was very satisfying. My wife had no idea I was experiencing this until I told her. We were both apprehensive about disclosing this to the mental health team. We need not have worried because she was very nonchalant and explained it was a common reaction - Robert

---

[43] (Graef, 1990)
[44] (Herman, 1997)
[45] (Herman, 1997)

Claire McDowall

2 POLICE CULTURE

Many Officers feel political correctness in the Police service is excessive and *"seemingly harmless remarks could now be interpreted as discriminatory"* (Loftus, 2012:64). They find it difficult to navigate everyday narrative and know what language is acceptable within a multicultural and diverse working environment. This has resulted in a *"subversive culture of resentment and discrimination bubbling underneath"* (Loftus, 2012:75). Diverse groups working within the Police service may feel unable to trust colleagues and feel isolated by them.

"The absence of discriminatory language is a consequence of a heightened awareness of the disciplinary line being taken against such slurs." (Loftus, 2012:63).

Rather than strengthen working relationships, perhaps through positive reinforcement, shared common experience in the role of Police Officer and building trust; the way in which institutions have implemented diversity strategies such as forcing compliance through the ever present threat of disciplinary action has perhaps further served to divide colleagues, deepen mistrust and affirm a 'them and us' attitude. These tensions in the workplace add to occupational stress for all concerned. Trust in colleagues in high risk situations is imperative, feeling 'threatened' by colleagues or the organisation, lack of comradery and sense of belonging and community contributes to PTS and PTSD.

What is common to *all* Police Officers is the potential for or actual experience of threat, verbal and physical abuse, 'normal policing duties' and the organisations default position on 'trouble makers' and complainants within the Police service. Perspectives on what it is like being a 'bobby' are shared by Officers regardless of ethnicity, gender and sexuality.[46]

Providing a service to a multicultural and diverse community also presents Police Officers with the challenge of understanding every member of the community they serve and remaining sensitive to ethnicity, religion, culture, mental health, disability, sexuality, gender reassignment and the needs of the individual when carrying out their duty[47]. Concern over complaints from the public is high[48] and this all adds to occupational stress.

Graef says that the introduction of PACE (Police And Criminal Evidence Act, 1984) resulted in Officers becoming more distant from the public and less inclined to get involved for fear of a complaint of rudeness.[49] Fear of reprimand and threat of disciplinary influences how Officers operate in their role.[50] *'Officers learn to 'cover their ass' to avoid disciplinary actions'* (Chan, 1997:79).

---

[46] (Loftus, 2012)
[47] (Code of Ethics, 2014)
[48] (Loftus, 2012)
[49] (Graef, 1990)
[50] (Loftus, 2012)

Therefore; history should teach us that the use of punitive measures can have significant negative consequences. These consequences are in conflict with the government's push for better 'community policing' and greater efficiency at a time of cuts and reform. As the majority of people in contact with the Police are deviant, Officer's must be stringently protected against the impact of false allegations. Providing Officers with recording equipment is recommended.

The Code of Ethics[51] and subsequent legislation to enforce the standards can be a positive tool for Constables to hold Supervisors and Police Staff accountable for behaviour which is in breach of the ethics. However; there is a likelihood that the 'code' could be used internally as a means to abuse power and authority over subordinates; particularly as scrutiny will come from within the organisation and not through an independent body.

Some degree of balance may be restored if lower ranking Officers are supported with whistle blowing and grievances. Constables need to have confidence in their ability to use the Code of Ethics to hold those with a duty of care accountable, or else the risks to their work environment, wellbeing and job security may be too high.

Researchers of 'Police Culture' and 'Police Personality' identify traits of depersonalization, alcoholism, desire for danger, cynicism, emotional detachment or lack of empathy, solidarity, authoritarianism, the Officer's 'sense of mission' and the concept of policing as 'crime fighting' opposed to service provision.[52] They attribute alcoholism, depersonalization, emotional detachment, cynicism, suspiciousness, deviancy, distrust and lack of empathy as

---

[51] (Code of Ethics, 2014)
[52] (Skolnick, 1966; Evans et al., 1993: cited in Coombe, 2013; Loftus, 2012; Atherton, 2012)

maladaptive behaviours to cope with the role of policing. The 'sense of mission' and concept of 'crime fighting' are motivators for people wanting to join the Police and this idea of Policing pervades throughout Police culture.[53] Officers watch for cues which may prelude violence.[54] The 'symbolic assailant' is recognized by the Officer according to their body language, style of dress and attitude (through use of language).[55] Therefore the Officer is hyper-vigilant to his/her environment and the potential for danger and threat. Skolnick says Officers develop specific ways of seeing their world and responding to it through distinctive 'cognitive lenses'. He believes the Police Officer role is comparable to that of a soldier.

Promotion within the Constabulary of people without leadership skills impacts on Police Culture and the relationship between supervisors and subordinates.

'...inappropriate selection and promotion...lead to the perpetuation of managerial style and behaviour ..[having] a negative effect on the...commitment of subordinates', 'research suggests... police employees work in a ... culture which... nurtures low commitment...' (Metcalfe and Dick, 2000)

Though researchers in criminology are interested in 'Police culture' and 'Police personality' they are inadvertently identifying traits, behaviours and coping strategies across the force nationally and internationally which are attributable to PTS; such as distrust, cynicism, alcoholism, hyper-vigilance, sense of mission and emotional detachment; therefore suggesting a widespread experience of post-traumatic symptoms amongst Officers and perhaps one which is intrinsic to Police culture and personality.

---

[53] (Loftus, 2012)

[54] (Skolnick, 1966), (Loftus, 2012)

[55] (Skolnick, 1966)

A study of 262 Dutch Police Officers, carried out by Carlier et al. (1997)[56] assessed PTSD symptoms at 2 weeks, 3 months and 12 months following a critical incident. 7% of Officers met full diagnostic criteria for PTSD and a much higher proportion of Officers (34%) suffered from significant subsyndromal PTSD symptoms. This is staggering when considering the study involved only 262 Officers and following a single traumatic event. If this was an average across a force strength in England and Wales of 128,351 Officers[57], this would suggest a parameter of the Policing population (based on this sample) of 43,639 Officers affected by subsyndromal PTSD and 8,985 Officers with full diagnostic PTSD following a single traumatic incident. Force strength in Scotland is currently 17,244[58]; this would mean approximately 5,863 Officers could be affected by subsyndromal PTSD and 1,207 could have full diagnostic PTSD. The research highlights that regardless of where the study was carried out within the context of the Policing community, the same considerations exist; such as symptoms and factors involved, including Trauma and dissatisfaction with Organizational support.[59] Their findings highlight the need for better Occupational Health strategies and interventions.[60] More research in this area would be beneficial.

Burnout is a contributory factor in sickness absence, PTS, Depression, Anxiety and stress. It can manifest when the individual is persistently asked by the organisation to perform duties which are in conflict with their own values (cognitive dissonance); combined with an overload of work,

---

[56] (Carlier, Lamberts, & Gersons, 1997:cited in Marmar et al., 2006)

[57] (Home Office, 2014)

[58] (Scottish Police Federation, 2014)

[59] (Carlier, Lamberts, & Gersons, 1997)

[60] (Carlier, Lamberts, & Gersons, 1997)

little or no control over how the organisation is managed or the impact of decisions on quality of service provision and the team. Lack of dignity and respect at work from colleagues and supervisors, loss of comradery or community at work and disappointment in ones' ability to help victims who are suffering, are significant factors in the development of burnout.[61] *"Burnout is a process, not an event"* (Farber, 1983b, p.3:cited in Salston & Figley, 2003).

Loftus identifies a hierarchy where some types of work are considered 'inferior' such as domestic abuse and neighbour disputes because they do not fit with ideas about what is 'proper' policing i.e. danger, excitement, action or fighting crime. She also highlights Officer's detachment and lack of sympathy when dealing with the public.[62]

Loftus discusses the recruits concept of 'proper' policing, 'sense of mission' and how seasoned Officers influence and reinforce these ideas within 'Police culture'[63]. There is less emphasis on the personal experience of the individual as a cause for the recruits adaptations to his/her work environment. It is perhaps reasonable to determine that personal beliefs and morals, workplace culture, personal experience, government initiatives, management style and the development of coping strategies all come together to create the 'police personality', 'police culture' and attitudes towards policing.

"…the cognitive tendencies of police officers may not simply be a result of on the job socialisation but also as a result of personality predispositions in those who apply for the job" (Reiner 2000: cited in Coombe 2013).

---

[61] (Salston & Figley, 2003)
[62] (Loftus, 2012)
[63] (Loftus, 2012)

When considering the Officer's attitude towards domestic abuse as a low ranking task and *"The masculine culture of the police …[influencing] attitudes and behaviours towards female victims of crime"* (Loftus, 2012:10) it is important to not only consider the orthodox heterosexual male belief system relating to this offence, but also explore how this type of task is often incongruent to the 'sense of mission' and concept of 'protecting the vulnerable against the predator'[64], which is so important to the Officer and his/her value in their role.

Cases of domestic abuse rely heavily on long term emotional and practical support to bring about successful conclusion to the violence and abuse and this result is not always guaranteed. It requires specialist support networks and largely relies on the consent and co-operation of the victim in bringing the perpetrator to justice. 'Policing by consent'[65] requires public participation, 'playing their part' in maintaining law and order and taking responsibility for their wellbeing and actions. There is a need for victims to willingly act on what the police say.[66] It therefore follows that the individual is expected to take on board advice given by the Police regarding their safety and assist the police by taking positive action. Having worked with victims of domestic abuse for ten years as a support worker; I can say it often happens that victims undermine safety measures put in place, by circumnavigating these in order to resume the abusive relationship or have contact, i.e. initiating contact with the perpetrator when bail conditions are in place prohibiting direct or indirect contact; thereby encouraging the perpetrator to breach bail conditions.

---

[64] (Loftus, 2012)
[65] www.gov.uk
[66] (Myhill & Quinton, 2011)

Police attending 'domestics' often find it difficult to identify a sole perpetrator and research shows cases involve reciprocal abuse and this challenges the concept of a clear cut 'victim' and 'perpetrator' persona.

Bristol University research 'Who does what to Whom'[67] says:- *'there were more than four times as many repeat incidents in the cases where both men and women were recorded as perpetrators than where they were sole perpetrators... A total of 400 incidents were recorded across the 32 dual perpetrator cases (compared to only 181 across the 64 sole perpetrator cases)'.*

The study highlights the difficulty at times to identify the 'primary aggressor'. Dr. Karpman's 'Drama triangle', when used to explain 'Frustration and Burnout'; highlights the roles we play as Victim, Persecutor or Rescuer. He explains that a persecutor thwarting attempts by the rescuer to save the victim results in the rescuer feeling like a victim.[68] The rescuer's efforts become wasted and pointless.

This could relate to a multitude of scenarios, i.e. the persecutor using manipulation and coercion to get the victim to resume their relationship. Repeated and persistent frustrations can lead to 'burnout' and mental collapse and the victim becomes perceived as ungrateful.[69] Dr. Karpman identifies five different 'drivers' portrayed in the rescuers role which are negative:-

❖ Be Perfect driver – Pride in the job gone. The individual focuses on completing tasks to perfection (which is unachievable).

---

[67] (Hestor, 2009)
[68] (Karpman, 1984)
[69] (Karpman, 1984)

- ❖ Be Strong driver – The individual pushes through difficult work and ignores or denies the effect on health because it is seen as 'weakness' to seek help. They are likely to stay in the job too long.

- ❖ Hurry Up driver – The individual makes themselves look busy and overworked.

- ❖ Try Hard driver – The individual starts a task with effort but does not finish it. S/he is exhausted because they haven't taken time out to re-energize. The individual then feels unable to recognise their achievements.

- ❖ Please Me driver – The individual relies on others to make them feel good about themselves and so seeks their approval by being a 'people pleaser'. Criticism is difficult for the people pleaser to take as they may feel rejected.

Herman discusses Traumatic Countertransference. The therapist (or in this case the Officer and rescuer) is affected by the victims' stories and accounts of trauma. She says the [rescuer] needs ongoing support to deal with their own reactions to this type of work. Emotional reactions can include identification with both victim and perpetrator and the individuals own capabilities to associate with the traits in both.[70] As Karpman highlights; we can move between victim, persecutor and rescuer roles.[71] The [Officer] can develop scepticism, minimisation, revulsion, disgust and judgment towards the victim.

When the victim does not behave in the way the [Officer] expects a "good" victim to behave, s/he may feel disgust and hatred for the victim and want to 'wash their

---

[70] (Herman, 1997)
[71] (Karpman, 1984)

hands' of them.[72] Domestic abuse is complex and I will not attempt to discuss it further here. However; it is useful for demonstrating disparity between public expectation of the Police and the reality of tackling this type of work, the potential for disillusion, burnout and adopting strategies of emotional detachment. The same may be said of other complex and emotionally difficult tasks, such as dealing with people affected by chronic mental ill health and elements of social welfare and duty of care. It is also important to say that the persecutor can be an offender, an organisation, a supervisor or a colleague who is un-cooperative. For example; a decision made by a supervisor which is not congruent with the Officer's efforts in dealing with a situation will most likely cause frustration and spark the victim state in the Officer. In high stakes situations the supervisors orders and actions could result in moral injury.

Controlling emotions constantly at work (habitual) means the Officer becomes unable to switch this control off in order to demonstrate appropriate emotion to victims[73] or people outside of work, such as family.

Loftus narrowly interprets her observations on female Officers. She believes they need to demonstrate masculine traits in order to conform with the culture and prove themselves.[74] However, the development of emotional detachment and an image of strength rather than weakness which are perceived as masculine characteristics, are consequences of the Police Officer role regardless of gender or culture.[75]

She describes Officers as antagonistic in the hope the individual will 'play the game' and fail the 'attitude test' by which the Officer is then in a position to arrest the

---

[72] (Herman, 1997)

[73] (Roberts and Levenson, 2001: cited in House, 2013)

[74] (Loftus, 2012)

[75] (Graef, 1990)

individual. If they are polite, compliant and co-operative the Officer is more likely to let the individual off with a warning and words of advice.[76] Skolnick implies the Officer may need to be antagonistic in order to generate a response in the individual which would warrant punitive action. This occurs when the Officer is not comfortable with penalising or arresting an individual for the presenting behaviour or offence. He says conflict between personal beliefs and the laws can create a 'painful state of opposing cognitions' and discrepancy between beliefs and behaviour.[77] Skolnick correlates this behaviour to the theory of 'cognitive dissonance'. He highlights the need for the Officer to adapt his/her beliefs or *"convince himself that the only way he could possibly make a living was by being a policeman"* (Skolnick, 1966:60). Many Officers feel they don't know how to do anything else but Policing and a change to a civilian role daunting.[78] This feeling is enforced by an institution which controls and dominates the individual, separation from community and feeling captive (albeit voluntary).

Graef highlights cognitive dissonance in 'Talking Blues'. He tells us Officers resent being used for political reasons when they are called in to 'Police' a situation; such as a protest and the public target the Police believing they are taking the government's side on political issues. Graef says Police Officers are subject to no win situations where they can't do right for doing wrong. They cannot avoid action and either course can result in a negative consequence.[79] *'Psychologists call this 'double bind'. And it drives people mad'* (Graef, 1990:17) Some Psychiatrists believe moral injury results from the individual's actions and decisions.[80]

---

[76] (Loftus, 2012)

[77] (Skolnick, 1966)

[78] (Kirschman, 2007:cited in House, 2013)

[79] (Graef, 1990)

[80] (Shay J. , 2014)

Throughout his book, Graef uses the analogy of GIs returning from Vietnam and being faced with public hostility and lack of support in response to their sacrifices when describing the experience of Police Officers.

He says he can think of no other example which comes close to the events of the era.[81] Written in 1990; he focused on events during the preceding decade, including the miner's strikes and riots (such as Brixton in 1981).

Officers still experience an ungrateful public in response to their attempts to rescue, protect and put their lives on the line for others in today's society. They are under scrutiny from supervisors, public, media and courts, particularly in relation to their responses in a difficult situation.[82] Discrepancy between thoughts, beliefs and expression, can be found in humour; used as a coping mechanism when dealing with trauma which Loftus refers to as 'Dark humour'.[83]

"sublimation, altruism and humour are the therapist's saving graces. In the words of one disaster relief worker, "To tell the truth, the only way me and my friends found to keep sane was to joke around and keep laughing. The grosser the joke the better." (Herman,1997:153)

'Canteen culture' and the ability to use humour is an important strategy for releasing tension. A common sense approach to freedom of speech in the force must be adopted. Researchers such as Waddington and Reiner have determined that Officers do not act in accordance with what they express and there is a difference between what they say and what they do.[84]

---

[81] (Graef, 1990)

[82] (Graef, 1990)

[83] (Loftus, 2012)

[84] (Loftus, 2012)

Most research in the field of 'Police Culture' has been based on direct observation of the Police at work and findings are predominately viewed negatively.[85] Experience has been open to the researcher's interpretation of what they see and hear at face value. Police behaviour and personality is measured according to civilian values and civilian expectations. This will not always transfer practicably to law enforcement and dealing with an unpredictable public.

Police Officers are *"not wired like civilians, they are 'hunters in a farmers' world... [and] cannot be treated like civilians in therapy – it just doesn't work"* (Lansing, 2012:14). Being unable to predict what they will come up against next means the Officer *"must be mentally and physically prepared for the ever-present potential for danger"* (Scaramella et al, 2011; Holdaway, 1983: cited in House, 2013). This behaviour signifies the potential adaptation of cognition demonstrated by hyper-vigilance and hyper-arousal in Post-traumatic symptoms.

Leadership and Management

Officers want leadership which rewards them with praise for good work[86] (which is sincere) and makes them feel proud to be a Police Officer and of the work they do.[87] 'Professional competence' in a manager is highly desirable; as this promotes a good image of the Police service to the public and colleagues, including sound ethics, quality service and strategy. Officers value leaders who encourage a positive attitude to work, increase job satisfaction and levels of commitment to the organisation; also known as 'Transformational behaviours'.[88]

Management skills have been found to be 'weak', particularly around motivating teamwork, communication,

---

[85] (House, 2013)
[86] (Mitchell, Stevenson, & Poole, 2001)
[87] (Dobby, Anscombe, & Tuffin, 2004)
[88] (Dobby, Anscombe, & Tuffin, 2004)

feedback to subordinates about work, supporting personal development, honesty and transparency.[89] A "command and control" system of management style is adopted[90] which is in conflict with the Officers need to have a sense of control over their work as a protective measure against PTS.[91] Commitment to the organisation and its' goals and investing effort in helping the organisation achieve those goals, are dependent on relations between employer and employee, whether the organisation is supportive or adopts blame culture and the level of leadership or management skills.[92]

There is a correlation between 'weak' management skills in its broad sense, poor working relationships, a culture that nurtures low commitment, lack of commitment to the organisation and sickness absence.[93] Commitment to the organisation and job satisfaction act as a buffer to post-traumatic symptoms.[94] Strong leadership protects Officers against the consequences of stress, increases morale and commitment to the role.[95]

The individual's experience of victimization by a persecutor (such as a supervisor, organisation or culture) results in 'burnout' and mental collapse.[96]

'Police supervisors, far from leading their officers into battle, are perceived as no more than disciplinarians… [and] are often viewed…. With distrust and even contempt' (Chan, 1997:91).

---

[89] (Metcalfe & Dick, 2000)
[90] (Metcalfe & Dick, 2000)
[91] (Mitchell, Stevenson, & Poole, 2001)
[92] (Metcalfe & Dick, 2000)
[93] (Metcalfe & Dick, 2000)
[94] (Mitchell, Stevenson, & Poole, 2001)
[95] (Maguen, Metzier, Inslicht, Henn-Haase, Neylan, & Marmar, 2009)
[96] (Karpman, 1984)

This has a direct impact on the Officer developing 'anxiety-avoidance' strategies as a means to 'stay out of trouble'.[97] Anxiety and avoidance are behaviours associated with psychological injury. King et al. says a malevolent work environment is the strongest precursor to post-traumatic symptoms; over and above combat, threat and atrocities.[98] Threat to life has less effect on post-trauma symptoms than other occupational and environmental factors.[99]

Good psychological health during and following trauma can be supported by supervisors who validate the Officer's feelings through acknowledging how difficult the task was and how well the Officer did in those difficult circumstances. Lack of acknowledgment will most likely contribute to a higher degree of Post-traumatic symptoms.[100] When the Officer denies or ignores their feelings about a traumatic event it can result in higher post-trauma symptoms[101] and so leaders and managers who offer recognition, praise and support will reduce the risk of the Officer developing PTS.

I heard two colleagues who failed to stop a man jumping off a bridge and killing himself were separated from each other as soon as they got back to the station and put in interview rooms. They were interviewed about the incident as if they had been at fault. They were not given any support, recognition for the traumatic incident or praise for how they had coped – Robert

In this example; the supervisors actions were unsupportive, un-empathetic, focused on a potential complaint rather than

---

[97] (Chan, 1997)

[98] (King et al.,1995:cited in Maguen et al., 2009)

[99] (Maguen, Metzier, Inslicht, Henn-Haase, Neylan, & Marmar, 2009)

[100] (Mitchell, Stevenson, & Poole, 2001)

[101] (Mitchell, Stevenson, & Poole, 2001)

the wellbeing of the Officers and demonstrated an accusatory stance. If complaints or disciplinary action occur, managers must be sensitive towards the traumatized Officer. To do otherwise would add to their stress.[102] A supportive organisation can protect against the development of post-traumatic symptoms despite where there has been exposure to a horrific incident and difficult personal life events.[103]

One Officer in 'Talking Blues' said the Royal Marine Officers looked after their men. When he moved to the Police he was grieved that Senior Officers looked after their own welfare and progression through the ranks; not the welfare of Police Officers. [104]

"anger and frustration at the organisation can produce significant and long lasting emotional distress" (Mitchell et al., 2001:44)

In light of new reforms recommended by Tom Winsor which involve funding cuts, fitness tests, changes to pay and pensions according to skills, efficiency and performance, increased public scrutiny and over 80% of the budget dedicated to employment;[105] the organisation must protect and care for its' greatest asset.

The organization as a potential perpetrator of abuse

There are clear indicators that the Police force has the potential and the power to be an abusive partner in the employer/employee relationship and where this is the case; the employee is most likely exposed to persistent and prolonged abuse, along with the feeling of no escape (save

---

[102] (Mitchell, Stevenson, & Poole, 2001)
[103] (Maguen, Metzier, Inslicht, Henn-Haase, Neylan, & Marmar, 2009)
[104] (Graef, 1990)
[105] (House, 2013)

for retirement). The individual adapts to an abusive relationship, a sub-culture, trauma and threat – contributing to PTS and resulting in altered behaviour. Robert described himself as feeling like an indentured servant and recalls spending years mentally counting the days or crossing days off on a calendar, until his retirement and his only means of liberation. He describes 'good bobbies broken' and others acquiescence to the doctrine 'you are just a number'. Officers can experience verbal abuse, intimidation, bullying, coercion, threats, manipulation, defamation of character, withdrawal of privileges, abuse of disciplinary procedure, obstructing transfers and career progression and isolation from colleagues, to name a few examples. Chan says whistle-blowers within the service are given the 'cold shoulder' and 'shunned' by Senior Officers and support is withdrawn.[106]

"Managerial ranks do not recognise that an unsupportive management style, and… blame culture can be alienating for [subordinates] and … impact on commitment. These findings are…. disturbing… [reflecting] the "command and control" systems" (Metcalfe and Dick, 2000).

Enabling factors

"The absence of public concern and political pressure to scrutinize the standards of police conduct means that there is little political risk for police organizations that ignore or pay only notional attention to police deviance" (Chan, 1997:82).

So how does a Constabulary enable abuse of power and authority? There is no contract of employment. The Officer is a servant of the crown and as such, has limited employment rights. Many employment rights available through UK law carry exemptions. There is no provision

---

[106] (Chan, 1997)

of a Union to represent Officers and offer protection from unfair treatment. The Police Federation does not have the power to act as a Union and can only negotiate and advise. These factors can give rise to an environment where abuse of power and authority can thrive. Power and control are gained through fear and psychological abuse; reducing the risk of challenge and confrontation. Therefore; the Constabulary has power and control over job security, working conditions and financial security.

Rank can be used as a weapon to enforce compliance, threaten disciplinary, allege insubordination, intimidate the individual, threaten repercussions and provoke isolation of the individual; labelling them as uncooperative or militant.

"They are intolerant towards people who challenge the status quo" (Loftus, 2012:ix).

When choosing to become a Police Officer; you are viewed differently by your community and may be rejected by that community.[107] Robert explained you are feared, hated or respected. Therefore; the Police Force becomes your community and in some cases, family. You may be led to believe no one else understands what you do or what it's like to be a Police Officer; creating a dependency on this relationship and the Policing community for social acceptance and belonging. Compassion Fatigue can contribute to withdrawal from others and the belief others would not be able to understand the effects of the difficult work of Police Officers.[108]

Withdrawal or expulsion from this community could see the individuals' social circle shrink. The identity of the individual and their self-image becomes synonymous with the identity and persona of the Police Officer. This is in

---

[107] (Coombe, 2013)

[108] (Salston & Figley, 2003)

part due to the public rejection of the individual within the wider community and the Officer never being 'off duty' to criminality and a responsibility to act. The Officer may keep their job hidden from social networks outside the Police because they don't want to be defined by their occupation.[109]

Invasion of privacy and the right to do so can become the norm, such as unannounced home visits during sickness absence, demanding access to the individual when they are off sick, getting colleagues to drive by the home address at intervals to check on the Officer's movements, or check on social media sites for any activity which suggests they are not genuinely ill, or persistent telephone calls during episodes of sickness absence; arguably deviant surveillance. Constabularies are known to behave this way, perhaps using duress to force an early return to work, perhaps to reinforce their power and authority. Deviant behaviours are used as a means to achieve the organisations goals, when following rules, policies, procedures and legislation prevent achieving this.[110] People have developed a culture now where there is an expectation that you will be instantly accessible or you will contact them back very quickly.

My mate from work couldn't even go for a shit in private without being pestered to answer the phone to his supervisor when he was off sick. Seriously, they kept phoning him when he was sat on the toilet. When he called back, he was chastised for not answering his phone.
When I was off sick for 24 hours, they kept calling and texting and when they didn't get a response; they came to my home and pounded persistently on the door. I never answer my home phone or have my mobile close by and I now know it is part of my PTSD. I didn't know they had been trying to get in contact – Robert

---

[109] (Coombe, 2013)

[110] (Chan, 1997)

Supervisors can be persistent in their attempts to make contact with you when you are on sick leave and failure to respond or allow this intrusion is often viewed as being non-compliant or uncooperative. It certainly is an invasion of privacy, or worse. If the Constabulary chooses to cite 'duty of care' and 'welfare' as reasons for an unannounced home visit; they must be able to demonstrate good grounds for doing so.

The organisation as persecutor, will likely elicit a victim response in the individual.[111] The Officer may often be denied autonomy, freedom of speech, the facility to make decisions involving the organisation or working practices, when or for how long they are allowed to take rest breaks and eat (reduced break times and no time to finish meals) etc. The culture adopts a 'do as I say, not as I do' attitude. In conclusion; boundaries and discipline are likely to be inconsistent, so the individual never knows what the boundaries and rules are. Working practices and creative interpretation of policy and procedure are adapted to the desire or needs of the supervisor, unless they wish to use policy and procedure as a tool for reprimand and punishment. These activities are controlling perpetrator behaviour. All these factors can result in the individual feeling captive within an abusive relationship and a loss of confidence to leave the relationship, the role and the Policing community.

Character, Temperament and the Police personality

In the case of Robert; he was always 'the first one through the door' on a job. He was proactive and encouraged a 'can do' attitude in colleagues. He dealt with unpleasant jobs for colleagues when they said they didn't want to do it; that they didn't like it. Even though he didn't like it either; he wanted to protect colleagues from trauma. He never 'cut

---

[111] (Karpman, 1984)

corners' on a job and always put in the effort to get the job done right. His character is one of generosity, empathy, intelligence, integrity and selflessness. He is motivated by 'justice'. He always pushed himself to get through difficulties or deal with jobs which he was uncomfortable with and he has high moral standards. His character fits Karpman's 'Be Strong Driver'.

He demonstrated this character through childhood; always determined to go to school when he was unwell and his mother wanted him to stay home and rest. His mother described him as always pushing himself to get on with things. He is far from fitting the description of someone who is a weak personality, character or temperament. He had a solid, happy upbringing as a child and comes from an 'unbroken' home which encouraged respect and honesty. The culture in which he worked was often more damning to him than the incidents he attended because he is an honourable man with strong beliefs about justice and the right way to treat others, working within a culture which (by his admission) largely does not share his beliefs and uses blame, bullying, intimidation and avoidance. He says he has seen many 'good Bobbies' break because of the way they are treated.

It is most common for people to cite their reasons for joining the Police as wanting to protect the weak from the predatory, a heightened sense of mission around the victim and a desire to 'make a difference'. Other attractions to the job are excitement and 'action'.[112]

The 'Rescue Personality' is under researched and so there is no firm evidence that such a thing exists;[113] however Dr. Karpman's Drama triangle (discussed in the section 'Police Culture') does identify behaviours associated with 'the rescuer' and negative coping strategies of this

---

[112] (Loftus, 2012)

[113] (Wagner)

persona. The 'Be Strong driver' which sees the individual reluctant to seek help, perception of weakness in doing so and subsequent denial that the situation is that bad[114] could explain (at least in part) the cultural machismo highlighted by Loftus.[115] This theory may contradict her notion that masculinity is forced on female Officers in order for them to fit in culturally and prove themselves. The macho (bravado) persona may be attributed to the dominance of white heterosexual male Officers as they make up the larger proportion of the frontline workforce and diverse groups have entered into this domain. However; there is a strong argument for the 'rescuer' personality having a strong influence on the presentation of Police Culture.

Susie Atherton, Senior Lecturer in community and criminal justice identified 'key characteristics' associated with Police Officers and looked for evidence of these characteristics in Police blogs[116]. These traits were cynicism, sense of mission (around victims), desire for risk taking, conservatism and solidarity. The Service element of Policing is largely considered boring by Officers and there is a strong desire for 'action-packed' activity and 'crime fighting' which makes a difference to society. [117] It is the overriding idea of what Policing is, both at recruitment and pervading throughout the Officer's career. It is attributable to the individual's reason for joining and how Police Culture reinforces this concept; particularly to probationers.[118] Loftus describes attitudes towards routine Police work as 'not proper Policing', exaggerated sense of mission and idea that the role is becoming more dangerous, despite the large majority of the Officer's time being

---

[114] (Karpman, 1984)

[115] (Loftus, 2012)

[116] (Atherton, 2012)

[117] (Loftus, 2012)

[118] (Loftus, 2012)

allocated to paperwork and community policing.[119] This attitude may be misunderstood as machismo, ego, over inflation of self-importance etc.

The psychological impact of the role on perception and behaviour needs to be taken into account. A behavioural response to burnout is 'boredom' and underperformance.[120] Exaggerated sense of danger is associated with hyper-vigilance and Post-traumatic symptomatology.

"[the] mixture of boredom and danger is a perfect recipe for stress" (Graef,1990:145)

"it is as if having lived in a world where the dice were constantly rolling, the calm, plan-filled responsibility of civilian life....is intolerable. They speak of it as "boredom". (Shay, 2002:45)

The Officers' 'sense of urgency' and impatience when dealing with work does correlate with what we know about PTSD symptoms of irritability, impatience and hyper-arousal and particularly the belief that the work is becoming more dangerous.[121]

Research into Emotional Dissonance in Police Officers acknowledged the need for Officers to regulate the display of their emotion in the role; thus suppressing genuine, real emotion and demonstrating emotions which are not authentic.[122] This has a negative impact on health and wellbeing; both psychological and physical. In order for the individual to cope with the emotionally difficult tasks; the Officer develops strategies such as depersonalization and emotional detachment. This results in an expression of cynicism, lack of empathy and dehumanization. It also sees

---

[119] (Loftus, 2012)

[120] (Salston & Figley, 2003)

[121] (Mitchell, Stevenson, & Poole, 2001)

[122] (Bakker & Heuven, 2006)

the Officer 'blame the victim'; just as Karpman highlights in the 'rescuer' role and the 'Drama triangle.'[123] Workload, organizational factors, poor supervision and management are the most significant contributors to burnout.[124]

"This may be disastrous for their performance: they may no longer achieve the objectives of their work, that is, providing high-quality service to ... civilians" (Bakker and Heuven, 2006)

An antidote to emotional dissonance can be found in good support from supervisors, including praise and feedback on difficult tasks and promoting pride in the individual for the job they do.[125]

Although the 'sense of mission' is present at recruitment; this ideology may become 'survivor mission' as the Officer becomes exposed to trauma. Judith Herman says personal trauma can be transformed into social action and through this action find meaning, i.e. helping others and protecting others from trauma or harm.[126] This may be why the 'sense of mission' remains consistent and as Loftus identifies, often 'exaggerated' in relation to the reality of normal policing duties.[127]

---

[123] (Karpman, 1984)
[124] (Brown & Campbell, 1990; Kop, Euwema, & Schaufeli, 1999:cited in Bakker and Heuven, 2006).
[125] (Bakker & Heuven, 2006)
[126] (Herman, 1997)
[127] (Loftus, 2012)

3 CONCLUSIONS ON POLICE CULTURE

Loftus concludes that 'dominant key features' of Police Culture remain unchanged by reform and the passage of time and orthodox Police Culture is still relevant today.[128] Suspicion, vigilance to cues of criminality, regular, persistent exposure to the 'darker sides' of society, resulting in an expectation of 'nothing but the worst' in people, detachment, cynicism towards supervisors and the public, sense of mission and a pervading sense of danger remain consistent.

There are arguments put forward by many researchers (such as Reiner, Westley, Cain, Skolnick, Punch, Waddington, Young and others) as to the definition of Police Culture, how it is formed and maintained and why it is resistant to reform.[129] Research explores Police Culture in relation to 'sense of mission', 'perception of proper Police work', a culture of 'masculinity', the effect of structural (organisational) conditions on lower ranks and the publics' expectations of the Police; an 'impossible

---

[128] (Loftus, 2012)

[129] (Chan, 1997) (Loftus, 2012)

mandate' which they continuously work to achieve.[130] *"The simplistic view that deviant institutional practice is caused by a deviant police culture"* (Chan, 1997:75) and more recently the individual Officers use of Police Culture as a 'toolkit' which can be drawn on to navigate unexpected and unpredictable elements of the job.[131]

Socialization of new recruits on how to behave and how to view their world as a Police Officer, adopting Police Culture and associated behaviour (such as machismo and suspicion) are argued to be the dominant reason for resistance to reform.[132] Loftus highlights the use of 'war stories' told by longer serving Officers.[133] Chan says this culture is a reference point for new recruits to draw on the experiences of others when faced with unpredictable work situations and Officers exert their 'choice' when doing so.[134] Westley identifies the persistent human degradation, evil and victimization to which the Officer is exposed; having an impact on Police Culture.[135]

Skolnick connects psychological condition and 'cognitive dissonance' as playing a part in behaviour and the Officer managing painful conflicting cognitions where there is discrepancy between what s/he is expected to do in their role and what they believe to be right. He also refers to Police Officers seeing the world through distinct cognitive lenses.[136] Though more could be said on Police Culture and research on this subject; there is not the scope in this book to discuss it further here. I have introduced this subject to demonstrate the potential interdependence between Police

---

[130] (Chan, 1997) (Loftus, 2012)
[131] (Chan, 1997)
[132] (Loftus, 2012)
[133] (Loftus, 2012)
[134] (Chan, 1997)
[135] (Westley, 1970:cited in Loftus, 2012)
[136] (Skolnick, 1966)

Culture and Post-Traumatic Stress, the gap in knowledge and understanding of the impact of psychological conditions on Police Culture, reform and public services and how reform, public service, organizational factors and job role impact on psychological health. The evidence suggests a possible large scale prevalence of symptoms across the force and research into this area is recommended.

There is disparity between the desire Officers have to provide a good service, be seen in a positive light and have pride in their vocation, with the reported low commitment of lower ranking Officers, lack of job satisfaction and affected levels of sickness absence associated with poor leadership and poor management skills;[137] and maladaptive behaviours to cope with the role of front line Policing, such as detachment and cynicism.[138]

Research into PTSD in Policing, health and safety issues, managing sickness absence and the impact of Policing on psychological health[139] are considered separately from Police Culture in its' broadest sense; including service provision, resistance to change, concept of proper Police work, relationships with the public and offender management. 'Police Culture', 'Police Personality', maladaptive behaviour and cognition which is distinctive to the Police Officer, correlate strikingly with the behaviours and cognitive functioning which are key features in Psychological injury and Post-Trauma symptoms.

Research into psychological health relating to Police Culture and vice versa is therefore an area in need of development and exploration. The previous chapters have highlighted there are several factors involved in

---

[137] (Metcalfe & Dick, 2000)

[138] (Patterson, 2003: cited in Coombe, 2013).

[139] (Mitchell, Stevenson, & Poole, 2001) (Hayday, Broughton, & Tyers, 2007)

Psychological injury and trauma. There is involvement in trauma, either personal or witnessed. There is persistent and prolonged exposure to the immorality and cruelty of people in the community, diminished community or sense of belonging or isolation. There is a sense of inescapable captivity, even if it has been entered into voluntarily (such as indoctrination into a specific culture), where the individual is subjected to persistent and prolonged abuse by those with power and authority. Finally, there is the failure of those with power and authority to do 'what's right' and failure to provide care and welfare in their role as provider and guardian (including employer with duty of care).

These components contribute to complex PTSD:-

- Trauma
- Societal immorality
- Vicarious Traumatization
- Compassion Fatigue
- Secondary Traumatic Stress
- Captivity
- Loss of socialization
- Moral Injury
- Poor leadership and organizational stressors

The following points are likely to affect the impact of occupational stress on the individual and the increased risk of being affected by Post-Traumatic symptoms:-

- Political correctness
- Burnout
- Increase in public expectations
- Decline in support and solidarity
- Policing in culturally diverse communities
- Low morale
- Service cuts and reduced resources

- ❖ Poor management and leadership
- ❖ Culture of blame and threats of disciplinary action
- ❖ Overly critical public, including complaints

One theme which has consistently appeared in research is the link between the organisation, how it constructs and manages the work environment, leadership skills, management style, support and welfare provision; with efficiency, effectiveness, attendance, commitment to the organisation and its' goals, quality service to the public and the presence of Post-Traumatic symptoms.

It has been identified that the malevolence or benevolence of the organisation is the difference between the development of Post-Traumatic symptoms and the protection against it. Thought needs to be given to what systems and strategies for engaging Police Officers will be successful. As one Officer says 'there's plenty of woolly fluffy stuff now if you want it'.[140] The Officer's 'be strong driver' must not be overtly threatened with 'touchy feely' interventions. Strategies could be covertly placed via strong leadership and supportive supervision, work environment, practices and personnel systems, regular supervision meetings, competent monitoring, review and risk assessment via Occupational health and raising awareness of symptomatology across the organisation. Dignity and respect, honesty, openness, positive reinforcement, personal development and abolishing deviant practices in managing Officers is imperative for psychological health.

Currently; the Police Force continues to adopt an antiquated mode of management. Positive reinforcement, encouragement and praise produces greater productivity and efficiency. Making mistakes must be viewed as learning opportunities and not punishable with blame and negative criticism. As people; we all respond better to kindness,

---

[140] (House, 2013)

empathy, dignity and respect. If an Officer is made to feel of no value or importance by their organisation; how can s/he be expected to value members of the public. If the Officers' concerns are not taken seriously or no one shows an interest in them; how is the Officer to care about the concerns of others. 'What you invest in the individual, you get back'. If you use deviant behaviour in line managing Officers; they will respond with deviant behaviour.

Constabularies would do well to adopt a 'menu of options' for support provision. One size does not fit all in relation to the type of support the Officer needs or feels comfortable with.[141] If your workforce is grounded in machismo; adapt your strategies to suit this group of people. Given that the evidence overwhelmingly points the solution to reducing PTS at leadership, management, supervision, organisational considerations, solidarity, job satisfaction and pride in the role; Constabularies should focus attention on getting their house in order regarding the treatment of their Officers as a matter of priority.

Provision of counselling, specialized counselling and critical incident de-brief should continue to be available and yet not the main strategy for post-trauma. Education within Constabularies (including Occupational Health) as to the causes of PTS and how they can play an integral role in preventing this debilitating condition[142] by using empathy, transparency, good communication, good practice, demonstrating genuine care about the wellbeing of Officers and can be trusted is imperative.

"*When the source of support and training is derived from the same source as the stress, the negative effects of work stress actually increased rather than decreased*" (Oliver and Meier, 2009).

---

[141] (Mitchell, Stevenson, & Poole, 2001)

[142] (Mitchell, Stevenson, & Poole, 2001)

The same can be said for counselling and other talking therapies provided or funded by the organisation. If the organisation is not trusted by the Officer; support from the same organisation will increase stress and be unproductive. Before effective treatment can begin; the Officer must feel safe and secure.[143]

Badge of honour

PTSD, Compassion Fatigue and Secondary Traumatic Stress demonstrates the Officer has fulfilled their role selflessly, passionately, compassionately and empathetically.[144] The Officer has not avoided difficult tasks or work situations. Their work ethic is most likely one that does not consider the limitations of safe levels of emotional and psychological experience. The individual pushes through the difficulties.[145] This character will have a tendency to stay in front line roles for the majority of their career.

Officers are routinely faced with the 'fight, flight, avoidance' response. This person is more inclined to face their fears, test themselves, stand their ground and rush headlong into a situation; not sit on the side lines watching or flee in the opposite direction.

Colleagues can be grateful to have this individual on their team. They volunteer for jobs no one else wants to do and buffer them against trauma; picking up work they say they don't want to do. They are likely thought of as trustworthy, reliable and efficient.

The achievements and sacrifices of this Officer must be honoured and communicated. There is no shame in psychological injury; it is a testament to the Officers' strength, commitment and sacrifice for others.

---

[143] (Herman, 1997)
[144] (Salston & Figley, 2003)
[145] (Karpman, 1984)

Claire McDowall

4 HOW MANY POLICE OFFICERS ARE AFFECTED BY PTSD?

Finding conclusive data on this issue is difficult. Police forces are not recording this information. All stress related sickness absence is being recorded as 'psychological disorder'; including bereavement, depression, generalized stress, family breakdown etc. The computerized data collection system does not have an option for recording PTSD.

Officers are not always disclosing their symptoms or seeking help via their Constabulary; many choosing private healthcare. This is likely to be partly due to distrust of the organisation and attitudes towards mental ill health in the force.

Data via Freedom of Information, submitted directly to various forces did not come anywhere near the figures anticipated, when compared with comments from a force psychologist, a recent survey and other research. Of the 1596 Officers employed by Norfolk constabulary in 2013,[146]

---

[146] (Appendix 4)

45 of those were off sick with a stress related condition and 51 police staff was recorded the same. Six Officers took early ill health retirement due to PTSD between 2009 and 2013. Only one Police Officer was referred by North Wales Constabulary for psychological assessment in 2013 and 2012. The number of Officers who sought counselling and welfare support in 2012/13 was 111 out of force strength of 1069 (full time equivalent).

The Metropolitan Police[147] were unable to meet my request because of the financial implication of retrieving information which was not recorded in a way which is easily retrievable and estimated 30,000 referrals for psychological assessment were made during the five year period. They estimate approximately 350 Officers took Early Ill Health Retirement due to Psychological injury for the same five years.

Thames Valley Police said no information was held in 2008 relating to psychological assessment. In 2009 there were 21 assessments, in 2010 there were 4, 2011-12 there were none and in 2013 there were 29.[148]

The Scottish Police Authority[149] were unable to answer the questions. West Midlands Police[150] did not make any referrals to a psychologist for assessment between 2008 and 2012. Seven people were referred in 2013-2014 and seven Officers were retired on ill health.

Mental Health NHS Trusts were contacted and all said they could not provide information on how many Officers had been diagnosed with PTSD or been referred for Psychiatry or Psychology services. They are not recording the occupation of their patients.[151]

---

[147] (Appendix 5)
[148] (Appendix 1)
[149] (Appendix 6)
[150] (Appendix 9)
[151] (Appendix 2,7,8)

Duty of Care

The following questions were asked of the Home Office[152]:-
1. Number of Police Officers (all ranks) who are recorded as taking sickness absence because of:-
a. PTSD, Post-Traumatic Stress Syndrome
b. Work related stress
c. Anxiety
d. Depression
e. Occupational stress
f. Stress
g. Any other mental health disorder or illness

2. Number of Police Officers (all ranks) who committed suicide or employment was terminated because of death by suicide.
3. Number of Police Officers (all ranks) granted Early Ill Health Retirement (EIHR) on the grounds of mental ill health.
4. Number of Police Officers (all ranks) applied for and denied Early Ill Health Retirement on the grounds of mental ill health.
5. Number of Police Officers referred for psychiatric or psychological assessment by the Police and the same for primary care?
6. Number of Police Officers receiving psychiatric or psychological treatment funded by the Police and the same through the NHS?
7. Number of Police Officers referred for counselling through the Police and the same for primary care?
8. Number of Police Officers referred for critical incident debrief by the Police?
9. Number of Police Officers referred for CBT (cognitive behavioural therapy) by the Police and the same for primary care?

---

[152] (Appendix 3)

The response from the Home Office FOI is as follows:-

The Home Office does not hold detailed information on the nature of sickness absence. The Home Office collects data on the number of Police Officers on long-term absence broken down by absence type, including certified sickness. However, further breakdowns providing the reasons for certified sickness are not collected. The Home Office also collects data on the number of Police Officer leavers broken down by reasons for leaving, including death. However, further breakdowns into the cause of death are not collected. The Home Office also collects data on the number of ill-health retirements. However, breakdowns providing the reasons for ill-health retirement are not collected.

The recent survey conducted by 'Blue Light Trauma Services', involving 350 Officers; was published on 'Policeoracle.com' on 1st October 2013.[153] The following results of the survey were:-

- ❖ Over a quarter of the study group are at high risk of PTSD
- ❖ 13% were signed off at least once with PTSD
- ❖ 51% were off for over four months
- ❖ 27% were assessed as high risk
- ❖ 21% were assessed as medium risk
  (Compared to 1.5% for the general population)
- ❖ There is a strong correlation to PTSD and long service, 3 quarters of the study group with over 25 year service were medium or high risk
- ❖ 64% never had critical incident debrief and only 8% said this was their force policy
- ❖ 80% said they did not feel their force was doing enough to support them.

---

[153] (Sommers, 2013)

The study identified a financial cost to the respective constabularies of the psychological sickness absence as:-

- ❖ Devon & Cornwall - £732,184
- ❖ Essex – over £1 million
- ❖ Staffordshire - £813,970
- ❖ Nottinghamshire - £439,151

It is not clear from the article what proportion of the group is working front-line or length of service front-line. There is no suggestion that episodes of physiological illness (relating to symptoms of diagnosed or unidentified PTSD) are included in these statistics; such as viral infections, asthma, gastrointestinal complaints, alcoholism etc. or other psychological stress, such as family breakdown, generalized anxiety or depression. Therefore; the impact on the financial cost, the strain on primary care services and the amount of sickness absence, attributable to Psychological Injury can be expected to be higher.

We can see from these figures that nearly half of those taking part in the survey are medium to high risk of PTSD. If this study involves only 350 Officers out of a workforce just shy of 130,000; it highlights the anticipated enormity of this devastating condition. HSE and Home Office research in 2007 into 'managing sickness absence in the police'[154] stated one force lost £7 million per annum on sickness absence and other force estimates indicated significant costs warranting the need for better occupational health facilities and research into the cost of mental illness specifically. The report also highlighted 'disability related absence was the least well monitored' and the Dorset 12 categories for recording the nature of the absence are too broad (as evidenced with the Freedom Of Information requests found in the Appendices)..

---

[154] (Hayday, Broughton, & Tyers, 2007)

The research has demonstrated a disparity between actual and anticipated cases of psychological injury and illness in Police Officers, (including referrals for Psychological assessment) with what is recorded officially. Therefore, these statistics are not being monitored and analysed.

An earlier book was published by Health and Safety Executive in 2001 titled 'Managing post incident reactions in the police service'[155] detailing research undertaken by the police Research Unit and Occupational Health Unit. The book provides a comprehensive schedule of strategies for reducing the risk of PTS and reducing the impact of this condition. Thirteen years later these principles of good practice have not been implemented on a 'real' and practical level and mental health issues have yet to get the same traction as other areas of diversity within the Police service.

---

[155] (Mitchell, Stevenson, & Poole, 2001)

5 GOOD PRACTICE GUIDE FOR CONSTABULARIES

The nature of the Police Officer role means it most likely the individual will be exposed to traumatic events. It is unhelpful for Senior Officers and the media to criticise Police Officers for claiming they have PTSD; expecting Officers to be unaffected by events and accept it's all part of the job. Police Officers are not genetically modified humans capable of resisting the effects of traumatic events and prolonged stress. They are normal people working in extraordinary circumstances[156] and deserve the respect and admiration of colleagues and communities for the work they do. There is much employers can do to reduce the effects of trauma and support individuals with PTS. A Health and Safety Executive report said:-

"pressures from workload, poor working relationships, daily hassles at work, and the atmosphere at work were all significantly associated with post trauma symptoms" (Mitchell et al., 2001)

---

[156] (Scottish Police Federation, 2014) (Graef, 1990)

"the importance of fostering a supportive and accommodating work environment... a compassionate work environment becomes a protective factor that …...shields police officers against the development of PTSD" (Maguen et al., 2009)

Unfortunately it is evident that PTS is still largely unrecognised by Constabularies as a problem or that there is a need to improve support to colleagues who present with mental ill health. *"Education of Officers at every rank is needed about work practices which can exacerbate or diminish psychological distress"* (Mitchell et al., 2001).

ACPO (Association of Chief Police Officers) highlights the 'often onerous', dangerous and stressful role of operational staff and acknowledges this may result in sickness absence due to stress or Post-Traumatic Stress. They go on to say managers have overriding responsibility for managing sickness absence in a sympathetic and supportive way and must comply with force policy.[157] ACPO state managers must *"Develop and maintain a system of managing sickness absence which minimizes the scope for inappropriate management or abuse of trust"* (ACPO, 2012).

It may be the case that these messages are not reaching regional Occupational Health, HR or Supervisors or there is no accountability for non-compliance with policy. Therefore, the printed word is 'fine and dandy' but of little use if it is not enforced or their application monitored and reviewed.

One area which is perhaps unexplored is the culture within civilian departments set up to support Police Officers in their role. HR and Occupational Health (for example) should operate without bias, in the best interests of the Officer and provide a service to Officers in accordance with legislation, policy and good code of practice. HR should act in ways which are fair to both the

---

[157] (ACPO, 2012)

organisation and the individual Officer; protecting both parties. These departments must advise managers and supervisors on appropriate practice in accordance with their relevant qualification, training and expertise. Senior Officers are not equipped to direct HR and Occupational Health issues.

The Police are seen as powerful. They have authority. To be in a position where you have power over the Police can open up opportunity for the civilian workforce to abuse power and control over Officers. Civilian staff have more rights (Union and Legal), the ability to control Officers' support and personnel systems, decide whether their pay is reduced, refuse the Officer Early Ill Health Retirement etc. When these departments are not held accountable or challenged about their working practices; they can become collusive and deviant.

Senior Officers may recognise the political power civilians hold over Police Officers at all levels and the threat of legal and industrial action. This may affect who has the greater authority over the Police; regardless of the status of civilian staff in the force i.e. lower level civilian employees.

Industrial action in 1989 by civilian staff had an impact on force efficiency; particularly as it involved support systems such as SOCO and communications.[158] A total of 78,513 Police staff (civilian) of which 13,552 are PCSOs were in post as at 30th September 2013 across the 43 forces in England and Wales. [159]

We were told by a psychologist that the organisation who contracts him; are actively and consciously ignoring or rejecting suggestions for improvement; saying 'we hear what you're saying but it doesn't fit with our organisation'. The suggestions for improvement and good working practice in this book already exist in the Constabulary

---

[158] (Jones, Newburn, & Smith.D, 1994)
[159] (Home Office, 2014)

policies and procedures and HR strategies. I am not expecting organisations to do any more than is already set out by legislation, policy, common sense and decency. Initiating and maintaining change in attitudes is primarily the responsibility of supervising Officers. Setting a good example to others is an expectation across the force.[160]

The pressure of work, and the lack of support from his colleagues and supervisors, had also become too much for him. My husband feels complete and utter deep-rooted bitterness and hatred towards the people in the police force who had a duty of care towards him, but who failed him time after time, despite the fact that they knew about the PTSD – (NICE Guidelines, 2005)[161]

What does high levels of sickness absence cost the organisation in terms of effective policing and financial implications? What does it cost the NHS and mental health service to support and treat Police Officers affected by mental ill health and PTSD? What is the cost to families emotionally, physically and financially? What is the impact on incidents of Domestic Violence? What is the impact on offending behaviour? How much is spent on Early Ill Health Retirement? How much does it cost Constabularies each year in psychology assessments and treatments? How much is spent on settlements out of court or at tribunal?

'Getting it right', early detection and intervention, preventative measures and risk management, eliminating blame culture and changing to supportive leadership are greatly more cost effective and better for everyone. It is a concern that Constabularies may be paying lip service to their policies and procedures and it is more common for them to work to unofficial procedures that suit their needs

---

[160] (Code of Ethics, 2014)
[161] (National Collaborating Centre for Mental Health Royal College of Psychiatrists', 2005)

as seen in deviant behaviour[162] and leaving Officers disorientated and unprotected. The following items and description on good practice are echoed throughout force policies,[163] HSE guidelines[164] and the HSE report on managing post-traumatic incidents[165] to name a few. In addition; I have drawn on my own experience as a line manager working for a housing association which adopts a 'person centred approach'. Those policies and procedures which are non-restricted or protected; are available online and in the public domain.

Perhaps the main areas where the Officer can be supported to reduce the risk of acquiring PTS or support the Officer who is affected by the symptoms of PTS are:-

1. Comradery in the workplace & Supportive and empathetic supervisors
2. Critical Incident debrief
3. 6-8 weekly supervision meetings (not currently an expectation)
4. Working to policy
5. Health and Safety Executive Management Standards
6. Transparency and integrity & Clear communication
7. Challenging the culture of bullying and intimidation
8. Health and wellbeing surveys
9. Person centred support

Comprehensive Occupational Health support and assessing for disability are covered later in the book.

---

[162] (Chan, 1997)
[163] (Critical Incident Debrief 'cldB' Force Policy, 2004) (Management Of Stress At Work Policy, 2007) (Managing Sickness Absence Procedure, 2007) (Managing Diversity; Dignity and Respect At Work)
[164] (Hayday, Broughton, & Tyers, 2007)
[165] (Mitchell, Stevenson, & Poole, 2001)

1. Comradery

Comradery has largely been lost within the police service and attitudes towards colleagues have changed. The threat of disciplinary, complaints from the public, complaints from colleagues and drive for promotion, have been highlighted as affecting behaviour by Chan,[166] Graef[167] and Loftus[168]. Unity, team working and colleague support is most often replaced with self-centred motives and self-serving actions and a blame culture. Comradery is important for increasing the feeling of safety and security; physically, emotionally and psychologically. A culture of comradery must be led by supervisors and by example. Some ways supervisors can achieve this are:-

- ❖ Avoiding favouritism
- ❖ Ensuring fair treatment to all
- ❖ Praise for great work
- ❖ Fair distribution of workload and types of duties
- ❖ Involving all team members in decision making and seeking their opinions
- ❖ Admit when you have made a mistake, take accountability and do differently next time
- ❖ Share your experience and what you have learned.
- ❖ Always treat colleagues with respect
- ❖ Take the concerns of colleagues seriously
- ❖ Be accessible and approachable
- ❖ Take positive action to bring about change for the better.
- ❖ Earn respect and trust
- ❖ Support colleagues through difficult situations with empathy and reassurance; rather than blame or criticism and acknowledge the difficult incident.

---

[166] (Chan, 1997)
[167] (Graef, 1990)
[168] (Loftus, 2012)

❖ Allow colleagues to influence change and the way the organisation operates.

Dr. Shay highlights the importance of keeping people together, send them into danger together and bring them home together as well as time to digest what they have been through together.[169]

Management decisions (which are often impractical) may induce low morale and resentment. One could argue that there is less sympathy for Police Officers with PTSD and that the police are mostly unsupported by their community. There is more likely to be a sense of apology for being a Police Officer and though there may be personal pride; the lack of national pride can contribute to a feeling that it is wrong to be proud to be a Police Officer.[170] This strengthens the need for comradery within the workplace.

2. Critical Incident Debrief & Mandatory counselling

What is the organisation's policy around Critical Incident debriefing following a potentially traumatic event? What is the referral process, including self-referral and who is responsible for what? If the organisation has a critical incident debrief policy; ensure it is made available and Police Officers are aware this policy exists during probation/induction, during team meetings/briefings and PDR meetings (yearly appraisal). Display a brief outline of the service available and how to make a referral on notice boards within Police premises. Ensure written invitation to attend group or individual debriefs are recorded and kept on Occupational Health records, including whether the individual attended. Written invitation and confirmation of

---

[169] (Shay, Odysseus In America: Combat Trauma And The Trials Of Homecoming, 2002)
[170] (Coombe, 2013)

critical incident debrief support is important and clarifies what is being offered and why. A written record demonstrates the organisation is acting responsibly and with welfare in mind. This should be recorded on Occupational Health records.

Does the organisation provide counselling support to Officers in specialist roles/departments such as Family Protection Unit? If counselling support is mandatory; ensure the Police Officer receives clear notification and appointment arrangements. Record the notification of appointment and attendance on Occupational Health records. The appointment should be rearranged if the appointment is inconvenient and a record made. Record if the Officer opts out of counselling on this occasion because it demonstrates the offer was made and the Officer exercised their right to decline.

3. Supervisions

Supervision does not take place except for yearly appraisal or an ad hoc 'chat'. The provision of regular supervision is strongly recommended. *"much secondary trauma can be avoided or its effects ameliorated [with] regular supervision or consultation"*(Cerney, 1995: cited in Salston & Figley, 2003). Clinical supervision is preferable because it gives opportunity to process distressing case details and emotions in a constructive way with a trained professional.[171] Implementing one to one supervision meetings to take place with each Officer on a 6-8 weekly basis with their line manager; may facilitate early detection of occupational stress. Each session will likely take up to 1 hour. With a ratio of one sergeant to eight Officers; this is a realistic goal.

Regular supervisions must explore workload and any necessary reduction or change or respite from certain types of work, need for micro debrief or counselling if any,

---

[171] (Salston & Figley, 2003)

mandatory counselling attended and dates available (specific to department), any noticeable change in patterns of behaviour, training and personal development needs, career progression, outstanding issues or concerns and an opportunity to make disclosures. Discussions and actions agreed must be recorded. A copy of the record must be given to the Officer to read, agree and sign. The Officer must have an opportunity to make additions or amendments. The importance of regular supervision cannot be stressed enough; in terms of monitoring the health and wellbeing of Officers. *"Denial and ignoring feelings about an incident are associated with higher post-trauma symptoms"* (Mitchell et al., 2001).

It is incredulous to consider Police Officers are facing extraordinary events; including life threatening situations, traumatic events, crisis management, direct abuse or violence and secondary trauma and yet receive no regular support or monitoring. This is even more striking when you consider other professions where regular clinical supervision takes place; such as for counsellors and support workers dealing specifically with second hand client trauma.

Far from being a paper exercise, there is real value in supervisions when they are conducted by good leaders who have the trust of their team. It is too often the case that this trust, rapport and comradery is not there and Officers feel unable to disclose any concerns for fear these disclosures will be used against them. Trust in the supervisors motives is essential.[172]

---

[172] (Mitchell, Stevenson, & Poole, 2001)

4. Working to policy (Welfare)

Policies are usually sound documents based on legislation and recommendations from professional bodies, such as the Health and Safety Executive, ACAS and Federation representation. Therefore; it is reasonable to expect Constabularies to follow policies and procedures set out for their organisation. The culture within the Police service is often to work to 'informal' procedures which have sprung up through deviancy and by example. Best practice is to refer to policies and procedure to ensure compliance with legislation; including human rights, equality and diversity. Working to organisational policies and procedures protects colleagues and the organisation as a whole, ensures fair treatment and respect and reduces the risk of bullying and intimidation within the organisation. It also protects the organisation from costly litigation claims.[173]

It is not appropriate for Constabularies to expect Constables to adhere to policy and procedure whilst supervisory ranking Officers are exempt from the same expectation.[174] Policies state they apply to all ranks. It is an abuse of power and authority to do otherwise.

Although policies are used for guidance; they are also stipulating legislative requirements and therefore breaching policy is potentially a breach of legislation. For the PTSD sufferer it is important for the organisation to work within policy and procedure. It helps with transparency and trust. It means both parties are working from the same set of expectations and rules. Working within set boundaries can afford some sense of security and assist in reducing confusion. Without clear expectations for both parties; it can result in the Officer having to 'jump through hoops' (which are unnecessary), feeling the goal posts are continuously being moved and lead the individual to believe

---

[173] (Employment Tribunal, 2014)
[174] (Code of Ethics, 2014)

there is cause for distrust. This behaviour is synonymous with an abusive relationship, where the victim never knows the rules, because there are no rules and as such, they will never be able to 'get it right'. No matter what they do, they are in the wrong and subject to blame.

5. Health and Safety Executive Management Standards

The Health and Safety Executive have identified the following factors affecting stress in the workplace[175] Organizations are advised to ensure these factors are addressed:-

Demands – the ability to cope with the demands of the job
Control – adequate opportunity to say how the work is undertaken
Support – adequate support from colleagues and managers
Relationships – not being subject to unacceptable behaviour
Role – understanding roles and responsibilities
Change – involvement in organisational changes

HSE research into managing Post-Traumatic incidents in the Police service (2001)[176] and Maguen et al.(2009) highlight a sense of satisfaction with the job and a commitment to it, associated with lower Post-Trauma symptoms and protection against symptoms; as does a sense of control over ones' work and organizational support. Other important factors are communication and consultation. 'Organisational characteristics' such as management and personnel systems are linked to levels of commitment to the organisation in lower ranking Officers.[177]

---

[175] (Management Of Stress At Work Policy, 2007)
[176] (Mitchell, Stevenson, & Poole, 2001)
[177] (Metcalfe & Dick, 2000)

6. Transparency and integrity & clear communication

Plausible deniability because of poor record keeping, keeping communication verbal and avoiding contact in writing is not conducive to an open, honest and transparent working relationship and lacks integrity. Police Culture sees written records often manipulated to prevent disciplinary action, 'ass covering' behaviour and avoiding review by supervisors.[178] There is a *"strong belief that there is little openness and honesty between ranks, thus fostering a defensive work climate"* (Metcalfe and Dick, 2000). The Code of Ethics[179] requires the Police Service to act with integrity, honesty and openness with the communities they serve. These behaviours must be habitual and therefore exercised with colleagues if there is to be successful transparency with the public.

Without evidence to demonstrate the employer or department passed on information, answered the question, provided the support and involved the Officer, the organisation will not be able to stand up to scrutiny when held accountable for neglect of duty of care. For this reason I would strongly advise to carry out all communication in writing. Where verbal contact takes place; this should be followed up in writing to confirm and clarify what has been discussed. For the individual suffering from PTS transparency and integrity are of great importance. Symptoms of mistrust, anger, confusion and self-harm/suicide can be exacerbated by a lack of honesty and common decency. When the employer behaves in ways which are obstructive, unsupportive and lacking transparency; this translates to an ulterior motive, underhandedness, bullying, intimidation, potential discrimination and abuse of power and control and increases the serious risk of harm to the Officer and their

---

[178] (Manning, 1977; referenced in Chan, 1997)
[179] (Code of Ethics, 2014)

immediate family members. An organisation which allows the individual to take a lead on their own care and welfare needs, follows policies and procedures, maintains accurate records and keeps the individual abreast of all communications in relation to them; demonstrates a concern for welfare, empathy and a desire to be supportive.

7. Challenging the culture of bullying and intimidation

It is unacceptable for Police Officers to be subjected to abusive behaviour by colleagues. Colleagues must support each other to get through difficult times and demonstrate they can be relied upon and trusted; particularly when these are the people you will be calling on for back-up in a sticky or life threatening situation.

Bullying and intimidation at the hands of supervisory Officers is even more unacceptable and it is important to hold people accountable for this behaviour (regardless of rank). 'Closing ranks' around a supervisor who has been accused of bullying behaviour or misconduct and colluding to deflect allegations would be misconduct in itself. This only serves to alienate and disillusion other Officers. The Code of Ethics requires Officers to 'Challenge and report' unethical or unprofessional behaviour demonstrated by colleagues; regardless of rank or role.[180] Bullying and intimidation must be tackled regardless of whether or not the abused individual has a protected characteristic. *All* Officers must be treated with dignity and respect.[181]

"Closing the curtains & hiding behind the sofa does not make it go away. People still know what is going on. You cannot hide incompetence, bad leadership or collusion" – Robert

---

[180] (Code of Ethics, 2014)
[181] (Code of Ethics, 2014)

8. Health and Wellbeing surveys

The organization can carry out health and wellbeing surveys[182] on a regular basis, to assess systems in place for identifying, managing and reducing stress; including the effectiveness of these systems. An action plan for improvement is created and implemented. Changes to operational systems are then regularly reviewed through further survey to measure the effect of the actions. Once standards of good practice are reached; the frequency of the survey is reduced to monitoring the maintenance of these standards.

An example could be identifying the need for early detection of psychological injury and the subsequent action could be the use of a screening tool. Another example could be surveys on return to work interviews, do they always happen, what was the level of detail and discussion, are risk assessments carried out, and are Officers happy with the standard of completion and supervisor support? What improvements could be made? Perhaps a survey or 360 degree feedback on the performance of supervisors, how approachable and supportive they are and how effective they are in their role.

9. Person centered support

The organisation must treat the Officer as an individual not a number. They must improve the working environment. The individual must be the lead on all decisions about their welfare and support and must be consulted on all communications, meetings, documentation and their options in an open, honest and transparent way.

"Trauma robs the victim of a sense of power and control" (Herman, 1997:159). In order to aid recovery; the individual must be permitted to take back their own control over their lives, their care and their employment.

---

[182] (Management Of Stress At Work Policy, 2007)

The individual must feel safe. To achieve safety; the Officer must not be re-victimized. Treatment cannot be successful unless safety has been established.[183]

"The SMP confirmed what I had known all along. My employer was the one who kept re-victimizing me and causing my symptoms to increase. I knew treatment would be pointless if I had not been able to first get stability in my life. They caused my irregular and reduced hours of sleep, my rage, my exhaustion and my hyper-arousal.

During periods where I had no contact with them I felt more stable, relaxed, positive and 'normal' so I saw the pattern of what was happening" (Robert).

Constabularies may re-victimize the individual through bullying, intimidation, abuse of power and authority, inflicting moral injury and captivity. There is a culture within the Police that Officers must follow direction without question. This attitude is not conducive to recovery or autonomy in the individual and denies the Officer his/her own power and control over their lives and their treatment. The Officer may perceive anything 'work-related' as a threat, including meetings with colleagues, communication with authority or their representatives, Police cars and Police premises.

Constabularies are most likely unaware of the trauma they can cause, the impact their actions have on psychological health and subsequently, how this exacerbates and re-victimizes the Officer, because people view PTSD as relating to a single traumatic event. This book aims to address this gap in knowledge.

---

[183] (Herman, 1997)

It is important for the individual to be stable before treatment begins, i.e. adequate sleep, sobriety and self-care.[184] Pressurizing the Officer to take treatment as a requirement of 'co-operation' with the force does not guarantee successful engagement with the process. The organization has a duty of care to minimize their impact on the individual and create 'safety'. If they wish the Officer to undertake treatment which they are willing to provide and fund, they must demonstrate professionalism and integrity if the individual is to trust the therapist who (in their opinion) is likely to be working for the 'enemy'.

Thomas V. Maguire, Ph.D.(1995-97) created a Bill of rights for trauma survivors. In the bill he encourages assertiveness in the individual to take leadership on their recovery and control over their treatment at the hands of others. For example; the individual is not answerable to anyone relating to their progress or who they have treatment or help from; neither do they have to justify their decisions. He says the individual has the right to challenge any action which breaches their boundaries or what is acceptable to them. It is appropriate for the individual to ask for explanation and clarification on any issue which is not understood. Should they disagree with the opinion of others; they have a right to say so and ask for any changes or adjustments which meet their needs.[185]

Re-Victimization (traumatization) of the Officer

The way in which the organization approaches, manages and supports the Officer is crucial for long term psychological health and wellbeing. As highlighted throughout this book; they are a key factor (over and above all other factors) in the protection against PTS and reducing

---

[184] (Shay, Odysseus In America: Combat Trauma And The Trials Of Homecoming, 2002)
[185] (Maguire, 1995-97: cited at www.safehorizon.co.uk)

the impact of PTS. Ann Jennings Ph.D. wrote an article titled 'on being invisible in the mental health system'; published in the journal of mental health administration.[186] Ann identifies the way in which the mental health system can re-victimize the traumatized individual through practice. The individual is unseen or heard, trapped, isolated, blamed and shamed, controlled, unprotected, threatened, discredited, betrayed and labelled 'crazy' by the institution. I have adapted this to Robert's case during long term sickness absence.

Unseen or heard	The force didn't believe he had PTSD or that he was genuinely ill. They ignored warnings of risk of harm. They did not discuss his wellbeing at monthly absence meetings. They didn't ask him what he needed or how he was affected.
Trapped	They are the key to his Early Ill Health Retirement(EIHR), Pay conditions and timescales for getting processes completed. They cut his pay against recommended practice. They delayed the grievance process, Psychology assessment, FMA appointments and the EIHR process.
Isolated	Left without wage slips for 4 months. No guidance on what to expect, policy or procedure. He was not told what conversations were taking place about him. Decisions were made without his consent or involvement. Documents were created without his input or agreement with the content.

---

[186] (Jennings, 1994)

Blamed & shamed	Robert was blamed for the actions of supervisors (relating to his grievance) and there was no acknowledgement of his mental state at the time of the incident.
Controlled	Robert was controlled through isolation, abuse of process and blame tactics. He was given directions without explanation and the organization resented his questioning of those directives.
Unprotected	Despite a diagnosis of PTSD and meeting the definition of disability, the force did not take into account his needs for adjustment to procedure, preferred form of communication and need for clear explanation and guidance. Their actions triggered stress and symptoms which put Robert and his family at risk of harm. The force did not operate within policy or legislation which resulted in discriminatory practice.
Threatened	Threats around non-compliance were subtle and aimed at getting control over Robert. Statements like 'ultimately, we must all abide by the rules' when Robert repeatedly maintained he could not cope with face to face meetings. Robert's privacy was breached at home on two occasions, with unannounced visits. The supervisors expected to gain access without prior agreement and their physical presence was intimidatory.

Discredited	Branded uncooperative and non-communicative. Grievance recorded as a dispute over 'management style' when it was about bullying behaviour. Ill health disbelieved until diagnosis of PTSD received after 6 months sickness absence. This diagnosis was then discredited when they said it was not 'formal' because it was the opinion of a Community Psychiatric Nurse.
Betrayed	Betrayal of 'what's right' by the organization and its' welfare departments. Cover up around the grievance, betrayal of trust with their actions
Labelled Crazy	Deviant behaviour to gain access to the property on many occasions, hidden agendas within email communication, keeping contact verbal to hide deviant behaviour. Comments which paint Robert as unreasonable – leading to paranoid feelings.

Distortion, Deletion and Generalization

The way information is managed and interpreted can say as much about organizational culture as it can about an individual. It is important for an organisation to understand and make meaning of information in relation to the individual, their disability and/or diverse needs.

Much of the communications from the Officer will highlight what they need, what they can do, what they can't do and how their normal functioning is affected. The organisation must seek out these details from the information they are given and not interpret communications as they would relate to someone with 'normal functioning'. The Code of Ethics[187] requires the organisation to consider diversity and the needs of those with a protected characteristic (such as disability). It also asks consideration be given to the person's vulnerability. Officers affected by mental ill health can be vulnerable. They may suffer from memory loss, confusion, suicidality, self-harm and changes in behaviour.

Federation representatives must bear in mind that they are likely to be supporting a 'vulnerable adult' and act accordingly.

If the organisation is unable to provide adequate and appropriate support to colleagues who have mental ill health, are vulnerable and/or disabled; their ability to do so for members of the public is questionable.

The following is a real life example:-

Officer's Statement	Organisations' Interpretation
I cannot cope with a face to face meeting with managers	He is refusing to meet managers
Robert is too ill at the moment. I will be dealing with contact until further notice, because he wants to keep lines of communication open.	1) He said he does not want any contact with the organization or the federation.
The grievance is about bullying and intimidation	His grievance is about 'management style'

---

[187] (Code of Ethics, 2014)

I would like all contact to be by email or letter and no phone contact at this time.	He's not communicating
Before I see the FMA to talk about adjustments at work; I need to see the psychologist for prognosis, recommended treatment and adjustments.	He said he doesn't need to see the FMA
I would like to rearrange the FMA meeting. I can't come to police premises. Can he see me at another venue?	He cancelled the FMA appointment

What picture is created by the organisations' interpretation and how they record this Officer's communications?

❖ He is refusing to meet managers
❖ He said he does not want any contact with the organisation or the federation.
❖ His grievance is about 'management style'
❖ He's not communicating
❖ He said he doesn't need to see the FMA
❖ He cancelled the FMA appointment

Suddenly we have ended up with personnel and Occupational Health records which demonstrate this individual as uncooperative and therefore not assisting the organisation, his recovery or return to work. This could affect employment rights and ill health retirement rights. The difficulties faced by the individual and the adjustments they require are not being considered. This could be taken as disability discrimination. Key points have been deleted such as 'cannot cope with' or 'rearrange' and the overall message is distorted. People use distortion as a way of constructing the outcome they desire in the future. Looking at the real life examples here; it is worrying to think that these distortions may have occurred to meet the organisations' desire to 'frame' the Officer as non-compliant, to blame, at fault, obstructive and uncooperating with the force.

If you find yourself in this situation; a lawyer will be able to advise you on what can be done. It may be possible to force the organisation to make amendments to personnel records and change the wording which has been used. It is advisable to raise complaints directly with the organisation about how information has been recorded and challenge their interpretations (by way of written correspondence). This will give you supporting evidence at court. Many Officers go to court unaware of what has been recorded about them. The organisation then produces personnel documents which portray the Officer negatively. They may label all the individuals' difficulties as 'personal' and not 'work-related'.

Constabularies will work hard to convince the Officer and other professionals that the difficulties are 'personal'. For example; if you disclose work-related PTSD and the force are aware of personal difficulties, such as bereavement and marriage breakdown, they will attribute the PTSD to personal trauma. Robert provided medical reports and a CPN letter which stated 'work-related' PTSD and they continued to say it was because of personal difficulties.

This behaviour deflects responsibility and duty of care away from the Constabulary and absolves them from any neglect of care which may have taken place. This strategy saves the force money. Pay conditions on long term sickness absence are affected. Pay need only be extended where the reason for absence is work-related, such as injury on duty (physical or psychological). Injury on Duty Awards can be substantial. If the injury is not work-related there is no chance of eligibility. If it can be argued that the disability results from a mixture of work and personal then the award is lessened.

Distrust and deception

There are likely to be times when the Officer will question whether they are becoming paranoid and imagining the hidden messages in communication, underhandedness, surveillance and psychological trip wires and booby traps. Are they (the organisation) trying to trip me up and catch me out?

When my husband first went on sickness absence and submitted a grievance; he made predictions on how the organisation would use deviant behaviour and his predications came to pass time after time..

It is heart-breaking to think Officers may be unable to fully advocate for themselves when dealing with mental ill health, stress breakdown, PTS and suicidal tendency at a time of vulnerability.

Home Office guidance on managing attendance states the starting point for managing sickness absence must be supportive action. *"Where police officers are ill or injured they should be treated fairly and compassionately"*. It goes on to say managers should be able to demonstrate they have acted reasonably at all stages of the attendance management process and complied with the Equality Act.[188] ACPO guidance places responsibility with managers to adopt systems which reduce the risk of 'abuse of trust'.[189] My husbands' distrust did not arise from paranoia. It came from experience. He had a long history where the organisation or supervisors distorted information and used

---

[188] (Hayday, Broughton, & Tyers, 2007)
[189] (ACPO, 2012)

blame tactics. He commented that they would rather put resources and energy into trying to 'catch people out' than supporting them and 'doing things right'.

Policy and procedure is often a one way street. Legislation, standards of professional behaviour and good working practices apply to all rank of Officer;[190] it is common experience that the policies and procedures only apply to Constables. Supervisors invent their own rules or distort policies to meet their own needs.[191] Supervisors are not usually held accountable or to the same degree as Constables.

It became a full time occupation to evaluate every message which came in, either verbal or written, to look for 'the trap' and the hidden agenda. One lawyer with extensive experience of this particular force commented that messages should not be taken at 'face value'.

The Officer must be made aware of their rights and entitlements by way of letter (such as appeal against decisions, annual leave, legal representation and injury on duty awards). None of these issues were raised with my husband or information provided.

"Following a meeting (which I did not attend) regarding appeal for an extension to my half pay, I was asked if I wanted to take my annual leave whilst on long term sick leave (12 months sickness absence); that it would demonstrate a good will gesture towards the organisation by reducing the impact on them and would benefit me because my pay would increase for four weeks. If I didn't use it I would lose it! How would the organisation benefit if they had to pay me more money for four weeks? After researching annual leave during sickness absence, I discovered case law had recently resulted in a change to police officer rights to get paid for all their unused annual leave on termination of employment or carry over the full amount to March the following year.

---

[190] (Code of Ethics, 2014)
[191] (Chan, 1997)

This information was not made available to me. You have to check every message, look for hidden agendas and assume anything they do is for their interests and not yours" – Robert

An incident of dishonesty occurred when Robert was due to meet with the SMP regarding EIHR. Robert was told an Officer would guide the Doctor to his home and then on to the motorway after the meeting because she did not know the local area. When the day arrived he not only escorted her to Roberts' home, but he fully expected to enter and gain access to a confidential medical appointment. This was an independent appointment from the force. There had been no prior agreement to this and the organisation did not disclose their intention to Robert. However they had disclosed their intention to attend the meeting to the SMP. The Officers' access was denied and the doctor agreed to carry out the meeting unaccompanied.

The Code of Ethics[192] requires Officers and Staff to refrain from misleading, inaccurate or false statements in any professional setting (either verbal or written). The organisation should have been clear about their intention to attend Roberts' medical appointment and their reasons for wanting to do so.

Good Practice Guidance for Occupational Health Advisors

Occupational Health and welfare are intended to be independent, unbiased and objective. They are required to take a lead on issues and advise Supervisory Officers. It is imperative that advisors avoid collusion with practices which are unlawful or cause the Officer exacerbated ill health and stress. Advisors must advocate for Officers and what is in their best interests. The welfare of the Officer and their family are paramount. Occupational Health

---

[192] (Code of Ethics, 2014)

advisors are key to supporting a change in attitudes towards the dignity, respect and treatment of Officers. Identifying PTS early means getting help early and reducing risks of harm, providing appropriate workplace adjustments and identifying disability (if any), provide support, reduce impact and reduce stress levels.

When staff repeatedly present with occupational stress and unexplained physical symptoms; ask the question![193] Give information on PTSD and ask whether they have experienced a traumatic event and give examples or a screening questionnaire. Education of Officers at every rank is needed to develop a greater understanding of psychological issues.[194]

"For patients with unexplained physical symptoms who are repeated attendees to Primary care... the primary care team should consider asking whether or not they have experienced a traumatic event, and provide specific examples of traumatic events" – (NICE, 2005)

It is not always evident when someone is referred to Occupational Health if the individual is experiencing generalized stress and anxiety, PTS or another condition because of many shared symptoms and it is not the responsibility of advisors to diagnose, nor within their specialism to do so. Occupational Health advisors should do explorative work around symptoms and how the Officer is affected.

A range of leaflets and sources of information should be available and given to the individual on types of workplace stress, including PTSD. There are many types of self-screening tools on line, leaflets and information available which advisors can provide Officers with or use as an aid

---

[193] (National Collaborating Centre for Mental Health Royal College of Psychiatrists', 2005)
[194] (Mitchell, Stevenson, & Poole, 2001)

memoir during conversations and meetings; for example 'Mind' have a leaflet on understanding PTSD, you can refer to the DSM-5 Criteria[195] which is widely available or refer to NICE guidelines.

There may be concerns within Constabularies that adopting these working practices could open the flood gates to people claiming to have PTSD, impact on the effectiveness of the service and the cost involved. This is not reason enough to recoil from making these changes, avoiding the situation or failing to provide support. Healthcare professionals are able to assess the authenticity of symptoms and this should give reassurance to constabularies in relation to fraudulent claims.

"Providing educational materials and raising awareness about post incident reactions does not increase the number of symptoms reported" (Mitchell et al., 2001).

Occupational Health must take an active role in assessing, monitoring and reviewing the wellbeing of the Officer. If a referral is received; it is good practice to screen for symptoms of Post-Traumatic Stress, carry out a stress assessment and take appropriate action. Occupational Health must lead on issues around mental wellbeing, advise supervisors (regardless of rank) on the best course of action and keep thorough, detailed records.

Where the Officer is on duty; Occupational Health must arrange meetings with the Officer and line manager to discuss adjustments to workload, type of work, working hours, change of department etc. Find solutions to reducing work related stress. Waiting for long term sickness absence before discussing recuperative duties is not in the interests of preventing serious ill health or managing the effectiveness of the service. Does the Officer consider

---

[195] (DSM-5 Criteria for PTSD, 2013)

themselves to have a disability and if so; what adjustments are needed in the workplace? The 'Job accommodation network' (JAN) has a page dedicated to the type of adjustments in the workplace which may be needed for the PTS sufferer.[196]

JAN suggests exploring what the individual requires within the following categories:-
- Memory
- Lack of concentration
- Time management
- Performing or completing tasks
- Disorganisation
- Coping with stress
- Working effectively with a supervisor
- Interacting with co-workers
- Dealing with emotions
- Sleep disturbance
- Muscle tension or fatigue
- Absenteeism
- Panic attacks
- Diarrhoea/vomiting/nausea
- Headaches
- Transportation

Some examples of the kinds of adjustments which may be required are; use of relaxing music, frequent breaks, driver to transport individual to work and to home, flexible hours, time to attend healthcare appointments, breaking tasks up into small steps, the use of an animal companion and personal work space.

---

[196] (Accommodation And Compliance Series: Employees With Post Traumatic Stress Disorder)

Occupational Health advisors must take an active role during the Officers' sickness absence. Occupational Health should not only get involved when the individual is ready to come back to work. To do so would result in many missed opportunities for support. There is a good deal of support the advisor can provide during the period of absenteeism; particularly around communication, medical assessments, information gathering, medical reports, disability assessment and adjustments to procedures whilst the individual is off work.

Communication during sickness absence can be difficult for the Officer experiencing Post-Traumatic Stress. Colleagues must work flexibly to ensure communication is facilitated in a way which is comfortable for the individual and at their pace, such as email and letter. Ensure information provided is clear and concise. Letters must include explanation and not just direction. For example; when arranging an appointment with the Force Medical Advisor (FMA); be clear what the meeting is for and who can accompany the Officer. Avoid ambiguous phrases. State specifically what is likely to be discussed.

During long term sickness absence; the Officer's day to day functioning may be altered and there may be difficulties which must be explored. This can be facilitated via a sickness review meeting or FMA assessment.

If information disclosed indicates difficulties in 'normal' day to day functioning; a meeting with the Force Medical Advisor must be arranged to assess for disability (If this has not yet taken place). The Force Medical Advisor must assess for workplace (psychological) injury. This will affect appeals against reduction in pay.

"I was told they wouldn't accept it was a workplace injury without a 'formal diagnosis' from a psychologist and I needed to prove it was a workplace injury for my appeal against reduction in pay. If this is policy; they should be arranging for every officer with psychological

injury to see a contracted psychologist in advance of the meeting to review our pay conditions - Alternatively; they should do what is set out in our sickness absence policy and allow the FMA to make this decision. I asked them where the criteria for a psychologists diagnosis was written in policy and they confirmed it was not written anywhere"
- Robert

Waiting lists for NHS assessment and treatment with mental health services; particularly with psychology services are very long. The organisation must refer the Officer to a contracted/private psychologist for capability assessment, prognosis and suggested treatment plan. The organisation must consider providing the Officer with private psychology services (including CBT) to assist in recovery and reduce the risk of serious harm. Where an Officer discloses difficulties with a traumatic event; Occupational Health, Welfare and the FMA must consider referring the Officer for Cognitive Behaviour Therapy (CBT) with a practitioner or critical incident debrief or EMDR (as recommended by NICE, 2005)[197].

The organisation must be aware of the various treatments available for Officers with Post-Traumatic Stress and understand counselling is not suitable for everyone and every circumstance. Counselling should not be seen as the only option for support[198] and if an officer declines counselling this must not be viewed as refusing to co-operate or that the organisation has fulfilled their responsibility to offer welfare.

Occupational Health and Welfare colleagues must update their knowledge on PTSD in order to provide the best advice and information to supervisors and Officers and work empathically with those affected. This can be

---

[197] (National Collaborating Centre for Mental Health Royal College of Psychiatrists', 2005)
[198] (Mitchell, Stevenson, & Poole, 2001)

achieved through reading, research, training and partnership working with mental health services.

Understanding the Onset of PTS

PTSD does not start immediately after a traumatic event and for Police Officers; it may not be related to one specific trauma. *"Trauma should not be thought of as a single stimulus".* (Mitchell et al., 2001).

It can take months or years for PTS to manifest or for the individual to understand the symptoms they are experiencing. Symptoms and coping strategies can develop gradually over time.

With my husband I got the impression that when he first had PTSD it developed quite slowly, but that while he was fighting it, it crawled into all the nooks and crannies – (NICE, 2005)

People tend to think PTS is caused by an incident which is catastrophic, such as a major disaster involving many people. However; research on behalf of the Health and Safety Executive (HSE), Managing post incident reactions in the police service; found 71% of 426 respondents in Strathclyde said memorable critical incidents were deaths of all types including murders, suicides and accidental deaths, such as road traffic collisions. 20.4% said other memorable incidents were threats to personal safety or dangerous situations and 4.4% said incidents of abuse or cruelty.[199] These types of incident are considered part and parcel of 'Normal Policing duties' because they are a persistent and frequent experience of operational front line Policing. Therefore; the potential impact of these incidents may be belittled because they are viewed as 'normal' when in actual fact exposure on this scale is beyond the realms of normal human experience.

---

[199] (Mitchell, Stevenson, & Poole, 2001)

The section on 'Barriers to self-identifying Post-Traumatic Stress' highlights some of the potential difficulties for the individual to know they are affected by PTS until the symptoms become intense, unmanageable, overwhelming or debilitating. It is not unusual to view PTSD in sterile, clinical terms and ignore the varying complexities and influences on the onset, the ability of the individual to know they are affected by PTS and the ability of the individual to communicate their symptoms to others.

It is not realistic to expect an Officer to know that increased anger, irritability, traumatic memory recall, withdrawal from others and unexplained physiological symptoms is attributable to PTS, without educating them on symptomatology or that the Officer will notice they have 'symptoms' and contact Occupational Health to disclose mental ill health in a 'matter of fact' fashion.

The Officer is more likely to present with physiological symptoms rather than disclose those related to thoughts, feelings and mental ill health.[200] The individual is likely to minimize and deny some symptoms. The Officer may be influenced by fear of disclosure to their employer, family, friends and health professionals for many varying reasons; not least of all because of symptomatic distrust.

Imagine you are coming to terms with the reality you have changed in ways you didn't expect, you fear you are going mad, you are having disturbing thoughts and feelings (beyond the norm), that people would say you can't cope or you are weak, that you could lose your job, lose your family or friends, lose your dignity and self-respect and your self-image/identity.

Asking someone to acknowledge they have PTS and make a disclosure is equal to asking someone to expose rawness, vulnerability and fear and to leave themselves

---

[200] (National Collaborating Centre for Mental Health Royal College of Psychiatrists', 2005)

unprotected and open to threat. Threat is one thing the individual is wired to detect and avoid. The Officer has diverse needs relating to safety and security around managing health and wellbeing, communication with Occupational Health and the organisation as a whole.

Working practice must demonstrate that the organisation can be trusted to care for the Officer, be non-judgmental, be supportive, do what's right, be transparent, be honest, put the Officer's needs first, adjust to the needs of the Officer and do things correctly. From this, comes the possibility of trust and therefore; the possibility there is no threat. The baseline for Occupational Health practice is to view the role as providing a quality service to clients/patients.

Good practice guidance for HR

Part of the role of HR Officers is to ensure the organisation works within policy, procedure and legislation; to protect the organisation from litigation and ensure employees are treated fairly, consistently and in accordance with these provisions. It is important for this department to advise other departments and management accordingly.

"HR didn't know what they were doing. They were complacent and lacked up to date knowledge on the Equality Act. They allowed themselves to be guided by Occupational Health and the Superintendent; and they didn't know what they were doing either" - Robert

Golden rules for organisations

Ensure you demonstrate and act in ways which are:-

Trustworthy - Trust is difficult for the Officer and must be earned; so demonstrate you can be trusted.

Transparent - Be open and honest in all communications

and be prepared to put advice and information in writing. If you are nervous about putting comments in writing or feel you want to avoid doing so; the chances are your actions are not professional, within policy or in line with standards of good practice.

Professional - Feeling safe and secure means knowing what to expect, the boundaries and rules. Personal opinion and prejudices must be side-lined. Follow policy and procedure, so both parties will be working from the same code of good practice.

Responsive - Respond to requests and contact from the Officer in a timely manner to reduce frustration, stress, distrust and isolation.

Accountable - Demonstrate a consistent approach across the organisation and ensure accountability is applied to all ranks and roles.

Person-centred - Demonstrate Officers are valued and cared for with words and actions, effort and service. Ensure welfare and support provision is led by the individual and their needs. Remember the welfare of the Officer and their immediate family are most important; not the organisation.

Responsible – Take responsibility for your role within the organisation and be pro-active in that role. Provide guidance to the Officer at every stage; not expect the individual to know what is required or to have the capacity to do so. Take responsibility for this process in the interests of reducing stress on the Officer, taking care of the Officer and ensuring all requirements are fulfilled.

Afford Justice – The Officer needs to know they are believed and their grievances are taken seriously. Investigate matters fully, listen to the Officer's anxieties and concerns, apologise sincerely, explain what you will do to ensure this does not happen again, listen to what the Officer wants and feels is appropriate resolution and where it is realistic; make it so.

Claire McDowall

6 ADVOCACY WITH YOUR EMPLOYER

Advocacy can be vitally important for the individual whose symptoms make it difficult to control emotions, behave assertively, write letters or emails with linear narrative and who are greatly affected by stress and flashbacks, memory loss and confusion.

Making a stand for 'what's right' (with determination) and how you are treated[201] is crucial for individuals; even if the outcome is not what you hoped for. The process is empowering and diminishes the feeling of victimization, powerlessness and subservience. It must be stated that this course of action will not be without stress and strife. Others who can help you, advocate for you and provide validation are lawyers, medical professionals, family members, federation representatives, charitable organizations and other support groups and advisors.

In her book 'Trauma and Recovery', Judith Herman explains that people are less likely to develop post-traumatic

---

[201] (Code of Ethics, 2014)

symptoms following even extreme trauma, if they adopt many of the following strategies[202]:-

- ❖ Take action, preferably with the support of others
- ❖ Avoid impulsiveness and taking action in isolation
- ❖ Stay calm and avoid 'reacting' (respond after giving thought to the situation)
- ❖ Stay true to your morals and values
- ❖ Find meaning and purpose in taking action (such as 'for the greater good' or 'justice') and the motivation to do so will be available. Communicate this to others
- ❖ Seek comradery and the protection of others in your actions (not collusion)
- ❖ Challenge orders you feel are inappropriate

My husband naturally operated in this way and demonstrated great resilience to the effects of persistent, long term trauma for 19 years of his career and personal events throughout his life.

We continued in this vain during his long term sickness absence which lasted over 16 months; during which time he was poorly treated by his Constabulary. Legal advisors described them, for all intents and purposes, as slow, incompetent, spiteful, short sighted and egotistical.

The Constabulary breached more than one legislative act and despite protestations of 'acting in the interests of welfare', they demonstrated none.

We communicated our concerns over the level of support which was given, procedures which were not followed, rights which had been overlooked and matters of disability which had been ignored. The organization was given countless opportunities to 'make good' and act professionally. At times we wanted to quit because it was exhausting and stressful. However; we knew we owed it to

---

[202] (Herman, 1997)

ourselves and colleagues to hold them accountable. For us; the prospect of rolling over and allowing ourselves to be victimized and treated thus would be catastrophic to our mental health. Knowing we had done our very best was incredibly important to us. Giving our difficulties meaning and purpose, enabled us to make sense of what was happening to us. Hence this book, sharing what we have learned with you and advocating for others where we can.

Personal journal

If I were to prioritize any action; it would be to write a personal journal of events from the onset. Log all verbal conversations, date and if possible, time.

Add entries immediately following conversations while the discussion is still clear in your mind. Put in as much detail as you can.

I found it useful to create a table on a word document. I logged the date, nature of the contact (email, phone etc.), who it was from or to and the content. I included emails on this index sheet too. I gave a brief account of the content and cross referenced the entry with a page number where the message was kept on file.

All copies of letters and emails were organised in a folder in chronological order. This was an invaluable resource and helped us to remember what had happened and when, what actions needed to be followed up and what actions had been completed.

It is also important to have these records for times when an organisation has no recollection of a conversation or has forgotten to answer a question. You can demonstrate when you asked the question and to whom you asked it. In the event you seek legal advice, submit a grievance or go to court; your records can be used as evidence and they will want a chronological break down of events.

It is far better and easier to update your records as you go; rather than try and organise this information at the end of your arduous journey.

Communications – (Reasonable adjustment)

It is a good idea to back up verbal conversations with email correspondence. This ensures all parties have a written record of what was discussed and an opportunity to correct, dispute or clarify any points.

Written communication is preferable. You haven't got to keep chasing someone for availability, email is instant and records the date and time the message was sent and when a response is received, it is a great source of reference for someone who experiences memory loss, encourages transparency and affords protection against deniability or disputes over who said what and one person's word against another's.

Written communication is more flexible. PTS sufferers can be up one day and down the next. Their mood is not always stable or conducive to holding verbal conversations. Emails and letters can be written and sent when the individual feels able to do so.

The other advantage with written format is that the letter can be crafted over hours, days or weeks, carefully considered and constructed. Verbal communication can result in further confusion, inability to retain the information, outburst of aggression, disrespect or bad language – ultimately resulting in insubordination. Written correspondence is as much about safeguarding the individual from 'getting into trouble' than anything else and should be considered a reasonable adjustment to someone with disabilities around social interaction and communication.

"The organization complained about using email. They said it is not the most effective way to communicate with me. 90% of their conversations and passing on information at work is done through email" – Robert

Robert was very isolated during his long period of sickness absence. Colleagues, supervisors and departments were talking to each other verbally and via email about him and never included him in any of these conversations.

It wasn't until he requested his records and all emails relating to him; that he became aware of what was being said (and assumed). Requesting to be copied into emails relating to you is a good way of keeping a check on any assumptions being made, correct information as appropriate and ensure welfare support is person centred (around you).

"My records and emails relating to me, all said I wasn't co-operating and every communication made me out to be obstructive. They even said I was off sick because of a grievance over 'management style' and disregarded my disability. If I had not requested these records; I believe they would have used this information to sabotage my employment rights or any court case" - Robert

Tackling organizational deviancy with logic and rationale

Illogical rationale and reasoning often accompanies deviant behaviour. These approaches are no match for logic, common sense and truthfulness. Sensible solution focused strategies and honesty will outwit deviant behaviour every time. Challenge arguments which make no sense and are not founded on fact. Keep emotion out of the scenario and concentrate on what evidence you have or can find through research. These skills will enable you to discover hidden motives and agendas. You will also maintain the higher ground in terms of legal action.

Your hyper-vigilance, heightened senses, policing skills and knowledge of how the force operates will help you sniff out ill motive. Asking questions and requesting explanation for the organisations' actions or inaction, are the 'test paper' by which you will discover level of competence, level of care and welfare and, their intention.

Know your policies and procedures

Your organisation's policies and procedures (non-restricted) are available via their website. If you have difficulty sourcing these; ask your employer to send you copies.

Perhaps the most relevant policies to you will be:-
- Managing stress at work
- Equality and diversity
- Sickness absence policy
- Management of Critical Incident debrief

In addition and dependent on your circumstances; you may also need:-
- Grievance policy and procedure
- Ill health capability
- Diversity, dignity and respect

You will most likely need to read the policies more than once to absorb the content, dip in to the policy as and when required and refer to it as you progress through procedures and long term sickness absence. Policies and procedures outline everyone's responsibilities and offer you protection from mistreatment.

Ensure you work within the policies; regardless of what anyone else does. Policies and procedures are based on guidance from ACAS, Health and Safety Executive and legislation. They are set out to ensure fair and lawful treatment and will guide you in terms of your rights.

"It was culturally accepted that supervisors used the policies as a stick to beat us with if we made an error and yet didn't follow the policies at all. They made up their own rules. We could be had up for misconduct or disciplinary and supervisors would get off with words of advice or no action taken. It is double standards" - Robert

Grievance

Grievance procedures are important. This is how organisations have an opportunity to develop and improve, build trust in their workforce, tackle situations causing stress and encourage resolution.

Some organisations deal with grievances better than others. It is always worth submitting a grievance and persevering through every stage of the process if you feel unsatisfied with the outcome. The more Police Officers do this; the greater the pressure on the organisation to make changes for the better.

"It is widely accepted that a grievance isn't worth the paper it's written on. You know from the start it won't go anywhere. I was at the point where I had nothing to lose; so I did it and kept going till I got to the Assistant Chief Constable" – Robert

If you are unable to cope with grievance meetings because of symptoms of PTS and you feel it unsafe to do so; ask your GP to write you a letter confirming this for your employer. Ask for the grievance to be dealt with in writing as a reasonable adjustment to the process. This is sufficient evidence that you cannot attend the meeting and should be accepted by the organisation.

"I maintained for 11 months I could not do face to face meetings, I provided a GP letter and the FMA highlighted I was emotionally unstable and confused in his report, I expressed concern around serious risk of harm to us all and they still would not accept it. Stage 1 of the grievance took 9 months to be resolved as a result and at Stage 2

they wanted a psychologist to confirm I couldn't attend a meeting. This was an attempt to undermine me and suggested I was lying. At this point I emailed the organization and said it was 'a disgrace' and 'an outrage' for which I was chastised"- (Robert)

Legal representation
This section is food for thought and provided as general guidance. You must seek professional legal advice around your personal circumstances.

Personal injury claim
You may be able to get compensation from your employer for PTSD. However; a word of caution.... It is very difficult to prove a Constabulary is responsible. You need to demonstrate:-
- ❖ The defendant was negligent
- ❖ That the negligence caused an injury to occur
- ❖ The injury was foreseeable (given the negligence)
- ❖ It must have been foreseeable that steps were necessary to prevent the injury

Other factors to consider are whether you have been tasked with a job outside your 'normal' role for which you have not received specialized training in preparation, not received adequate support (including counselling or debrief) or you may have communicated to your line manager that you felt the job would cause you trauma.

"My colleague Nigel, on response was asked to investigate indecent child images. Our Sergeant told the specialist department for this job that his team would deal with it. Nigel refused, saying it would traumatize him. The Sergeant insisted. Nigel spoke to his fed rep who backed him up and told the Sergeant he could not force anyone to do this job. The Sergeant argued and said 'he's a police officer; he cannot pick and choose what he does'; to which the fed rep told him if he persisted it would go to tribunal." – (Robert)

This is an example of where an Officer was tasked with a job outside his 'normal' duties, for which he had no training and could have foreseeably resulted in trauma. Policy supports Nigel's choice to decline and highlights the need for adequate training and support and the potential for the individual to be traumatized.

Discrimination claim

As a servant of the crown (not an employee) your rights within employment law are with exemptions. However; you do have rights and it is advisable to seek counsel from a specialist lawyer who understands police regulations.

You may have a legal case if you can demonstrate discrimination in relation to a protected characteristic; such as disability. Seek advice from your legal representative.

Employment Tribunal – Useful facts

- ❖ The Tribunal panel are not restricted to a limited compensation award in a discrimination case. Figures awarded can be large and unpredictable. A large pay-out combined with public and press exposure raises the risk for the organisation opting not to 'settle out of court'.[203]
- ❖ The organisation can still put forward an offer to settle the case out of court on the day of the tribunal (last minute settlement).[204]
- ❖ Employment Tribunal is a civil remedy. Decisions are based on a balance of probability.[205] This is why it is so important to record events and communications, gather supporting evidence and always behave appropriately; meeting your obligations according to policy.

---

[203] (Employment Tribunal, 2014)
[204] (Employment Tribunal Hearings)
[205] (Employment Tribunal, 2014)

Workplace Injury

The Force Medical Advisor (FMA) can assess you for workplace injury for the purposes of establishing appropriate pay conditions and if they believe you are eligible for EIHR (Early Ill Health Retirement) on grounds of disablement from 'normal policing duties', they can refer you to an SMP (Selected Medical Practitioner).

"I had a diagnosis of work related PTSD (injury on duty) from the Community Mental Health Team and the FMA. The organization did not accept the diagnosis and insisted on diagnosis from a psychologist or psychiatrist; even though the sickness absence policy says the FMA can assess for disability and workplace injury; yet they never arranged for me to see the contracted psychologist prior to my reduction in pay" – (Robert)

Injury on Duty Award

You can apply for an injury on duty award at the point of retirement, on grounds of permanent disablement of 'normal policing duties' or once you have left the force. Consider whether you have good grounds to make the application. There are no guarantees of an award. You can make the application via your Personnel/HR services.[206] If your organisation does not send you information on your rights to make this application; request this directly from them.

The SMP will be asked to complete an assessment of your future workability and potential earnings. S/he will place you into one of four bands following assessment. The amount you will be entitled to will depend on the degree of disablement, earning capacity and any subsequent loss of earnings. For example; your ability to undertake alternative employment and any shortcomings in salary compared to

---

[206] (Police Pension Scheme Injury Award Procedure: Injury Award Procedure, Version 9., 2010)

your existing wage. The SMP will determine whether your disability is slight, minor, major or very severe. This will dictate what percentage of average pensionable pay will be guaranteed (according to length of service) and the gratuity as a percentage of average pensionable pay[207]. They will also take into account whether the EIHR was a result of work related issue only or if personal issues are involved. This affects the percentage you would be entitled to. If you are using a solicitor; they can assist you with this application and EIHR.

Annual leave during long term sickness absence

Any policies relating to annual leave and sickness absence, prior to 2013 may be out of date with changes taking place to Police Officer rights via legislation.

Essex and Gwent Police forces (amongst others) have published their updated policies on-line in relation to the Working Time Regulations and you may find these useful to reference. Annual leave continues to accrue during long term sickness absence. You can request to take accrued annual leave during sickness absence if your GP provides a Fit Note to say it will not affect your health and recovery. An example may be a holiday abroad. Your sickness absence can then continue after this period of annual leave.

If accrued annual leave has not been taken during a 12 month period of sickness, it will be carried over to the next leave year in full. This will automatically be added to your annual leave entitlement for the following year and can be used up till the 31st March that year. Your Constabulary may still want you to make a request to carry this over even though it is not a legal requirement; so check with your force area.[208]

---

[207] (Police Pension Scheme Injury Award Procedure: Injury Award Procedure, Version 9., 2010)
[208] (Annual Leave Policy and Guidance, 2013) (Essex, 2013)

"Although there is a legal right to carry over this leave, any request to do so must be forwarded to the Head of Service Area to allow for authorisation of requested periods to be granted" – *(Gwent Police)*

If your employment is terminated (for any reason, or by either party), any unused and accrued annual leave will be paid. If your employer does not carry over annual leave or pay for annual leave on termination of employment; you should seek legal advice and consider action through an employment tribunal.

Appeal against reduction to pay

If you have suffered a psychological injury at work; it is advisable that the organisation extends full pay and avoids any reduction during sickness absence.

Carry out your responsibilities in terms of recovery and cooperation; otherwise the organisation may be entitled to reduce your pay. However; this does not mean foregoing your rights and wishes or acquiescing to the demands of the Constabulary if their instructions or requests are in conflict with your needs. Provide regular GP certificates, attend healthcare appointments, keep the organisation updated on treatment and recovery etc. Policy is likely to state financial hardship is not reason enough to extend pay; however the organisation must be mindful of the impact of financial stress on the Officer with PTS and their family and consider that this person may be a 'vulnerable adult'.

If the organisation has not arranged for you to see the FMA to assess you for disability and/or workplace injury prior to reduction in pay; I would advise you request this appointment via Occupational Health by email or letter.

The FMA can assess you for workplace injury and disability which will influence the outcome and inform the appeal process.

"My appeal was declined. They said I was still off work because of a grievance; though they knew I was due for a psych assessment. They didn't send off for my GP medical report, arrange for me to see the FMA or carry out a sickness review meeting prior to the appeal. I had complied with my responsibilities. I was suffering from complex PTSD after years of service to the crown and my community, I was suicidal and we had financial stresses at home. My pay was cut. When asked if I could appeal again following my psych assessment with a CPN; they said yes but insisted on a formal diagnosis from a psychologist and there is a long waiting list to see one on the NHS"- (Robert)

Getting your employer to understand your circumstances

PTS is largely stigmatised by people with no experience of the condition or what it is like to live with the symptoms. It is often seen as a non-entity, a fabrication and a way of getting compensation.

One of the aims of this book is to challenge people's ideas about PTS and start taking it seriously. Living with PTS can be nightmarish. The more Police Officers talk about it, open up about their experiences and hold their employer accountable for their treatment and health and wellbeing at work; the greater the chance of bringing about change and better working conditions. Dealing with traumatic events is inevitable in the Police service. This does not mean comprehensive support is not appropriate, needed, valuable, necessary or voluntary.

Much can be done to raise awareness of the issues. With over 128,000 Officers dealing with traumatic events on a regular basis across 43 forces in England and Wales, over 17,000 Officers across Scotland and approximately 7,000 Officers in Northern Ireland;[209] it is expected that a considerable number are experiencing occupational stress

---

[209] (Police Service Strength, 2013)

and symptoms of PTS. There is strength in numbers and the greater the number of employees raising concern and awareness; the greater the understanding and certainly acknowledgment that greater understanding is needed.

This is an issue for ex-Police Officers, those on long term sickness absence, probationers, those unaffected by PTS and those who are likely to be affected at some point in the future.

Prevention is better than cure:-
- Encourage a culture where PTS is openly discussed.
- Tell people about this book.
- Ask your Federation Representative to get involved locally and nationally
- Ask for information on this issue to be posted on notice boards or sent via email.
- Use social media as a forum for getting discussion going.
- Ask for what you are entitled to such as critical debrief meetings, recuperative duties, monitoring and review of health and wellbeing.
- Hold your employer accountable and responsible for your welfare.
- Expect welfare support in practical terms and not just in gesture.
- Expect your human rights to be upheld.
- Set up a workplace forum for occupational stress and PTS. Ask a Fed Rep to attend the meetings. Nominate a chair and take an active role in influencing and negotiating change.
- Know what to expect by referencing policies and procedures and request these actions are done. For example; ask for a sickness review meeting, ask to see the FMA, ask to see the contracted/force psychologist for assessment, ask for the workplace injury to be recorded, insist all relevant information is gathered prior to reduction in pay etc.

HR and Occupational Health records

You are fully entitled to request copies of all your HR, Occupational Health and Welfare records and any emails relating to you which have been sent by colleagues and supervisors. You may be charged a small fee for copies. I strongly advise making this request because you can a) provide your solicitor with records confidentially b) check what conversations are taking place in relation to you c) check you are happy with what is being documented; including people's personal perceptions and any disability discrimination.

"I heard by accident that Occupational Health said I wasn't co-operating or communicating. This sparked my request for my records. This was the best thing I could have done. I was able to directly challenge the organisation" – (Robert)

Accountability

The culture of accountability is obscure at times within the Police service and this can contribute to 'moral injury'.

According to policy; rules, legislation and standards of professional behaviour set out in the organisation policies, procedures and Code of Ethics; accountability applies to all ranks. However; this very often does not work in practice. In order for Officers to feel protected and safe, to know their grievances will be taken seriously and to be afforded justice; the organisation and its employees at all ranks and in all positions must be held accountable in a fair and consistent way.[210] I propose four ways to achieve this:-

1) For all Police Officers to assertively advocate for themselves and their rights and continue until they are satisfied with the outcome; even if this means legal action or involving your local MP – The greater the number of

---

[210] (Code of Ethics, 2014)

people doing this; the more the organisation will need to make positive changes and listen to what you are saying.

2) Unite together to speak as one. If an entire shift come together with the same grievance and can provide examples and evidence; the organisation is more likely to act to resolve the problem and hold the person accountable.

3) Call for an independent body to audit, inspect and review how grievances are dealt with and their outcome; audit, inspect and review Occupational Health and HR services and use powers of authority to hold the organisation accountable for collusion or corruption of processes, neglect of duty, breach of legislation or Code of Ethics and organisational failings.

4) Ask for greater employment rights, in line with the general workforce and comparable to Civilian Staff.

Request a sickness review meeting
(For long term sickness absence exceeding 28 days or when reaching the trigger point on the sickness absence score)

A sickness review meeting is held when the trigger point is reached for long term sickness absence or there is a serious concern for the wellbeing or welfare of the individual.

If the organisation does not initiate this meeting; I would advise you request one is held via your line manager. Roberts' complaint to the organisation that no review meeting had been held, despite reaching seven trigger points (such as Bradford score, diagnosis of Depression, Diagnosis of PTSD, phone call from family to the Inspector; stating his mental health was deteriorating etc.); resulted in amendments to the sickness absence policy. It is now force policy that meetings should be held monthly, not ad hoc and at the discretion of supervisors.

The meeting is an opportunity for you to explain how you are affected by your ill health, what support you need from the organisation, what they can do to enable a return to work (if appropriate) and what adjustments to procedures you believe you need during sickness absence or once returned to work.

If you are unable to attend the meeting because of the nature of your sickness absence; you can submit a written statement which details the information you want to impart and the information you are requesting. A representative can attend the meeting on your behalf to advocate for you. I would also recommend providing the organisation with a letter from your GP stating you are unfit to attend the meeting.

Some of the items the organisation may wish to explore are:-
- Patterns of sickness absence
- Anticipated time-scales for improvement
- What action the individual has taken to assist their recovery and return to work
- To establish whether there are any factors in the workplace, contributing to absence or ill health
- Support the organisation can provide (if any)
- Any work/environmental adjustments which may improve the situation
- The nature of the job duties causing difficulties
- The outcome of any previous return to work interviews or sickness review meetings
- The outcome of any referral to the Force Medical Advisor
- Any domestic difficulties, medical or work problems affecting you
- The prognosis and time scales for improvement
- Whether you may be fit to undertake duties at some point in the future

- ❖ Possible recuperative duties (if appropriate) and/or the outcome or review of any existing recuperative duties action
- ❖ The likelihood of future recurrences of sickness absence or ill health; including frequency and duration of anticipated episodes
- ❖ Whether the individual should be considered for a temporary or permanent move to another job
- ❖ Whether the individual may have a disability defined by the Equality Act 2010 (EqA) and any reasonable adjustments that may be necessary

The organisation can take into account your views on these matters and may wish to have the opinion and recommendations of the Force Medical Advisor.

Both the organisation and the FMA will likely require a psychology report to inform decisions on a return to work. This should not impede conversations at a sickness review meeting as to what adjustments and support you need from the organisation during sickness absence. It is an opportunity for you to make your employer aware of any matters you want to highlight. This could be risk of harm, the need to have contact with the organisation via written correspondence or that you believe you have a disability as defined by the EqA.

A sickness review meeting is one of the main ways your employer can ensure they are in possession of the most correct information relating to your sickness absence. This is because you are involved in this communication and providing information directly to them.

A sickness review meeting may be the most appropriate way of sharing sensitive personal information, recording this information and agreeing an action plan.

The outcome of the meeting may cover:-
- ❖ Further monitoring
- ❖ Further review meetings
- ❖ Referral to the Force Medical Advisor
- ❖ Referral to Occupational Health and Welfare Department
- ❖ Restricted duties
- ❖ Reasonable adjustments
- ❖ Recuperative duties
- ❖ Medical redeployment
- ❖ Consultation with HR Services
- ❖ Ill health retirement

It is important for the organisation to hold a sickness review meeting prior to reducing the Officer's pay after six months as it will inform the process, clarify if the Officer has co-operated with the force, whether the sickness absence is in relation to a workplace injury (psychological injury) and whether the FMA needs to assess the individual prior to the reduction in pay. A sickness review meeting should be convened as soon as the organisation has identified the individual has a disability as defined by the EqA (see 'A note on disability', P.151).

If you believe you have a disability; tell your employer in writing and ask to see the FMA. For suggestions on the kind of adjustments you might want in the workplace; see The 'Job accommodation network' (JAN). You can find information at www.askjan.org/media/ptsd.html

Force Medical Advisor appointment

If the organisation does not initiate a meeting with the FMA and you feel it is appropriate to have one; ask Occupational Health for an appointment and highlight what you want the meeting for. This may be to assess you for disability, fitness for work, workplace adjustments, workplace injury or referral to a psychologist.

Contracted psychologist

Write to your Occupational health department and ask if they have a contracted psychologist or the services of one. If you have applied to the NHS for assessment or treatment and there is a long waiting list; it is advisable to request an assessment via the Force. It will most likely be a 'capability assessment' (Caps) and in accordance with questions posed by your employer; such as ability to return to work or return to 'normal policing duties'. A 'Caps' assessment will set you back approximately £900 privately. Expect that your Constabulary is unlikely to pay for treatment via the psychologist and more likely to opt for 'specialized counselling'. Treatment is provided by a counsellor trained in CBT and/or EMDR. You may prefer to see a psychotherapist or psychologist and have to make these arrangements privately or via the NHS. The important thing is that you undertake treatment which you feel comfortable with and feel you can engage with, with a degree of trust. Otherwise the treatment will be unproductive, disappointing and will not induce disclosure.

Recording meetings (Reasonable adjustment)

Ask your fed rep to use a voice recorder during meetings and provide you with a copy on disc or take a voice recorder with you if you attend. Be open about the presence of the device and place it in view. Explain that you need to document the meeting in this way because minutes of meetings are not comprehensive and you need a detailed version of what is said as a consequence of the PTS. This may be because of confusion, memory loss or distrust. This method will most likely protect you from bullying and intimidation throughout the meeting and will provide you with a record of the verbal conversation.

Early Ill Health Retirement (EIHR)

People may be reluctant to tell you that you are unlikely to be redeployed or that you will be unable to perform 'normal policing duties' again in the future. You may be met with diplomatic responses about recovery and return to work. Even if the organization is thinking you won't be coming back; they will not communicate this without the opinion of the FMA, Psychologist's capacity assessment and SMP (Selected Medical Practitioner) report. If trauma is work related; it is very possible that policing will throw up triggers to symptoms and relapse in the future. In addition; behaviour associated with PTS can be unsafe in a confrontational work environment. Your ability to return to work will depend on your individual circumstances and to what extent you are affected by ill health or disability.

You can request EIHR; though it is best to do this at the opportune time. If you request this too early; it may be refused. You first need supporting medical reports. Ensure you have a psychologist's capability assessment first. Your employer should organize and fund this for you; so request this appointment if it isn't forthcoming. This assessment will explore the severity of the symptoms, treatment, prognosis for recovery and capability to undertake normal policing duties. These medical reports will assist the SMP with his/her decision.

The FMA will meet with you for a review of your circumstances and the psychologists' report. He or she will then prepare their own report and recommendations for your employer. Should they agree that EIHR is the best course of action; you will be referred to the SMP, which is a requirement set out by the government to protect employees against unfair dismissal. The SMP is an independent GP. The SMP report is then considered by the head of HR and a decision made.

Beware: it has been known for the Head of personnel to refuse a referral to the SMP even when it has been recommended by the FMA and the force psychologist has said the Officer can no longer perform normal policing duties (as in Roberts' case). It defies common sense and logic and can cause further stress to the Officer and their family. Similarly; the recommendations of the SMP for EIHR may be refused. The decision rests with the head of personnel, not the SMP. EIHR should be agreed when there is adequate medical evidence to support it. There should be reasonable grounds for refusal. Leave nothing to chance.

When you receive a letter concerning EIHR asking you if you are happy to proceed; giving you an option to request other information or comments are taken into account; assume they will only refer to the SMP report unless you specifically ask for them to consider other reports, such as FMA and Psychology assessment.

"Unless you spoon feed them specific information or requests; they will not use common sense and initiative, include other documents, join the dots and communicate with each other effectively" Robert

You can request support from a lawyer with the EIHR process. The lawyer can make recommendations to the federation that they fund an independent medical report for you to strengthen your case for EIHR. Your lawyer can appeal against the decision against EIHR on your behalf through crown court.

Please note: If you receive a letter refusing referral to the SMP or refusing EIHR; you have 21 days to lodge an appeal with the court. Robert received a letter refusing referral to the SMP and was unaware of the appeal process because no explanation was given as to his right to appeal or the deadline for this.

Deviant behaviour in the organisation

Behaviours to be aware of and watchful for are:-

- Absence or lack of information on processes & procedures
- Failure to provide information on right of appeal or delaying the information; limiting the time for appeal.
- Avoiding written communication
- Determination to have access to you in person or over the phone when this is not appropriate.
- 'Cherry picking' information in order to distort and delete messages.
- Declining to answer reasonable questions
- Requests and messages which contain a degree of illogical rationale and hidden agenda
- Schmoozing – 'I look forward to seeing you get back to doing the great job you do. You're a good cop'. (not taking needs or complaints seriously)
- Utilizing your Federation Representative to meet their needs as an organisation and act in ways which are devious.
- Omitting to tell you about benefits which may be an advantage to you; such as application for an Injury Award or option of referring you to see a psychologist

Claire McDowall

7 LIVING WITH PSYCHOLOGICAL INJURY

Coping strategies and Safety strategies
Coping strategies are behaviours which help the individual to function day to day. For example; relaxation techniques, changing negative thoughts into positive thoughts and visiting the place which causes anxiety, thus challenging, confronting, reducing or controlling the symptoms. This is known as 'active problem solving strategies'.[211]

I decided a good strategy for me was to retrain myself to stop looking in cars at the occupants. If I saw someone I didn't like the look of or who had attitude, it would set me off – (Robert)

Safety strategies are behaviours which support the anxiety. Our emotions (the feeling of flight, fight or avoidance) can direct our actions. When we feel these emotions it is a warning to us that we need to take action to avert some kind of threat or danger. Rather than assisting the individual

---

[211] (Regel & Joseph, 2010)

to overcome the source of the anxiety; Safety strategies involve avoidance, flight and suppression, such as use of alcohol or substances, social withdrawal and avoiding places and people.

These behaviours do not help the individual to recover and improve their quality of life. These are called 'avoidant thoughts and behaviours'.[212]

It was in the afternoon and the Doctors surgery was occupied by elderly patients and the odd teenager engrossed in their mobile phone; logically I knew there was no threat. I couldn't stop scanning and my anxiety became too great. I left and went straight home – (Robert)

A therapist may be able to help you develop coping strategies (new helpful behaviours) and reduce distress. In the first instance you should consult with your GP who can make referrals for you to the mental health team. The mental health team can assess you and direct your treatment from there. This will most likely be a referral to the community mental health team (CMHT) for assessment. The assessor will then refer you onto appropriate treatment such as Psychology or Psychiatry. NHS waiting times may influence your decision to seek advice through private practitioners. If you choose this option; ensure the practitioner is accredited.

What does PTS say about me?

People often worry this means they are weak or will be perceived as weak. They may also feel guilty and worry they have let people down in some way. For Police Officers who hold values around protecting others, their responsibility towards others and providing for their family; these emotions can be very strong.

---

[212] (Regel & Joseph, 2010)

What does it say about me if I experience PTS?
- ❖ You are an amazing person.
- ❖ You deal with often unpleasant, tragic and dangerous events which others would not choose to do.
- ❖ You have provided a service to your community and your colleagues, affording people protection and putting others first.
- ❖ You are human like everyone else, you may have more resilience than most and you can burn out too.
- ❖ You may become exhausted and you deserve help and support
- ❖ It demonstrates you are honourable, dedicated, compassionate, selfless and courageous in your role as a Police Officer.

What does this mean?
- ❖ It's okay to ask for help and support.
- ❖ You have strength, courage and perseverance
- ❖ You and your contribution to our communities is valued and appreciated
- ❖ It's okay to be kind to yourself and think positively about your achievements
- ❖ Taking time to care for you means you stay healthy and are better able to help others.

Measuring PTS
I will not explore how to measure the intensity of the PTS. I would like to highlight a different kind of measurement.

My husband and I were frustrated that literature on the subject of PTS tended to be based on members of the public who had experienced a single traumatic event such as a road traffic collision, or focused on combat stress in the military. His experiences and factors involved in his PTS didn't compare well with the single trauma and seemed more akin to combat stress.

He felt that comparing his experiences with veterans and those still serving would not be wholly appropriate. This was partly out of respect and partly because policing is a different experience.

There was a period of trying to find where he sat comfortably and he commented that there is always someone who has dealt with worse. He minimized and belittled his own experience. He does not feel worthy to compare himself with military heroes and at the same time acknowledges he has been through a great deal. In my years working in domestic abuse I would often hear clients say the same thing about the degree at which they were abused. Many felt guilty for being at refuge because they felt they hadn't suffered enough to earn a place there, especially when there had been no physical violence. If this sounds like you; I want you to acknowledge your experiences and the impact this has had on you with no guilt or comparison with others and remember that policing has challenges unique to this role and you are Blue Light Heroes.

Police Trauma Spectrum

Whether you are affected by stress, depression, anxiety, PTS, complex PTSD or any other psychological condition brought on by policing; your mental and physical self are affected by symptoms to a lesser or greater degree.

There is a danger that Officers fail to 'join the dots' and build the big picture of what is affecting them. A person may notice each symptom in isolation. When the Officer does not have 'flashbacks' they assume they are not affected by PTS, even though many other indicators are apparent.

Remember that the PTS can creep up on someone without their awareness. Physiological symptoms may come and go without explanation and psychological symptoms are likely to be perceived as normal in relation to the role of an Officer.

It may not become obvious until a stress breakdown occurs. In some ways it can appear that PTSD lies dormant until a significant impactful trigger manifests full blown symptoms following all the warning signs that were already there.

The term 'stress' in Post-Traumatic Stress Disorder can be misleading. Symptoms are the result of hyper-arousal and maladaptive behaviours. Workplace stressors are a major factor in the development of PTS and repeated persistent exposure to horrors are significant.

Stress is a word which is used so frequently and in so many different situations that it's meaning has been somewhat diluted. When someone says they are suffering from stress, it is not taken as seriously as befitting persistent Police trauma. The word 'stress' minimizes the experience of the individual and contributes to the belief that the person is weak and cannot cope.

I would advise all Officers to be mindful of changes in physical or mental health and behaviour which repeat, are persistent and unexplained (particularly lethargy and tiredness). Consider that these may lead the individual from the lower spectrum of work related stress to a higher spectrum of Complex PTSD. Seek help as early as you can to reduce the degree at which you are affected by stress, hyper-arousal and trauma and improve recovery.

Risks associated with Post-Traumatic Stress

Triggers for anger are not always known to the Officer. Therefore; episodes of explosive anger may not be predictable in any given environment. Anger and rage can be indiscriminate and the person on the receiving end can merely be in the wrong place at the wrong time.

- ❖ There is a risk of violence towards family members, members of the public and colleagues
- ❖ Some individuals may find there is a risk of road rage and therefore risks are increased when driving.

- ❖ Increase in alcohol intake
- ❖ Self-harm and/or suicide
- ❖ Committing a criminal offence (involving an act of violence or dangerous driving)
- ❖ Reckless behaviour and no regard for personal safety or consequence (such as dangerous driving or sexual promiscuity).

Potential impact on family life and relationships
- ❖ Family breakdown, separation and divorce
- ❖ Infidelity, sexual promiscuity
- ❖ Violence or abuse
- ❖ Withdrawal from family and friends
- ❖ Withdrawal from social activities and events
- ❖ Little or no patience with children and/or partner
- ❖ Tension and stress
- ❖ Anxiety and symptoms of PTS can be inherited/adopted by partner or children (compassion fatigue)
- ❖ The family may become alert to mood changes in the individual and feel there is unpredictability; perhaps a feeling of walking on egg shells

Self-actualization
How can PTS affect self-esteem, achievement, outlook on life, drive, purpose and all that underpins the ability to reach self-actualization and full potential?

Individuals can suffer from low self-esteem accompanied by feelings of guilt, shame and thoughts about self-weakness and world sorrow.

Self-image is likely to be altered. For example; someone who has always been active and goal orientated finds it difficult to set goals or take steps towards achieving the goal, suffers from lethargy, exhaustion and depression and struggles to get motivated to do things. The individual may increase alcohol intake, require medication and longer periods of sleep. There are many ways in which self-image

can be affected by the symptoms of PTS. Some other examples of self-image which may be challenged are the individual as:-
- Carer
- Provider
- Parent
- Friend
- Member of the community
- Husband/Wife/Partner
- Employee and employable
- Someone with a career
- Protector of others
- Useful and helpful
- Planner/organiser
- Respected
- Desired

Achieving a sense of normality in life and meeting basic needs can become the main occupation; Such as, the extra time and effort it can take to do everyday tasks which others take for granted.

PTSD left me feeling impotent in the sense I could no longer provide for or protect my family or be of use – (Robert)

It may take longer to get up, washed and dressed, prepare food, go to the supermarket, organise finances and may be extremely difficult to hold down a job, socialize or carry out tasks independently outside the home.

In some cases; the individual becomes 'cared for' and there may be some tasks with which help is needed; at least for some time during recovery. Financial security may be at risk where job loss occurs and this can impact on other areas of life; such as homelessness and debts.

Values and priorities may alter as a result of traumatic experiences. For example; where once material gain was of great importance, now good health and security take precedence. Less is taken for granted and the simple things in life are more appreciated. Traumatic events can call into question our mortality and in turn a re-evaluation of what is trivial and petty and what must be most respected; i.e. life giving and life sustaining factors such as shelter, comfort, food, safety and security. This may be one reason why the individual has little or no patience for 'small talk' or the perceived petty squabbles or moans and groans of others.

The individual is wired for survival and all other activities may be categorized as extraneous.[213] This explains many behaviours and symptoms, such as memory loss, withdrawal from others, hyper-arousal and hyper-vigilance.

Lifestyle choice

It is important to feel a sense of purpose, to be active, involved and occupied and at the same time make allowances for relaxation, rest and reflection.[214]

It may be difficult to do as much as before and you may be challenged to look at your roles and identity differently (as highlighted in the section 'self-actualization'). This can mean adapting to a new idea about who you are as a person. Rather than feel negatively about being unable to meet expectations, take this opportunity to be unconventional, focus on your skills, talents and interests.

I spent over half my adult life as a police officer and it had become my identity; after all you are never really off duty and have to forfeit some rights to individuality. As a police officer you are hated, feared or respected and this can make integration with others outside the force difficult. – (Robert)

---

[213] (Shay J., 2014)
[214] (Regel & Joseph, 2010)

So you can't make it to the supermarket or the shops? Shop online and get stuff delivered. You feel more comfortable visiting the bookstore so do this activity instead.

So you feel it's not viable for you to go back to work. You feel you would be under pressure to achieve in this environment? Go self-employed. Perhaps turn your hobby or interest into a business. Work the hours, days and times you want to or perhaps take early retirement and pursue interests you never had the time to before. Perhaps undertake a distance learning course or degree. Re-label yourself as 'self-employed', 'author', 'writer', 'blogger', 'volunteer', 'student', 'house-husband' etc.[215]

Some things in life need to be planned, appointments made and activities organised. It is okay to let everything else happen as and when you are in the mood to deal with it. Some people prefer to know exactly what is taking place and when, planning their weeks in detail. Others prefer a more relaxed attitude to life and go with the flow. If planning ahead is difficult for you. 'Cross each bridge as it comes', instead of projecting yourself into the future. It is also worth considering that plans can change at short notice; whether we have control over it or not. Therefore; keeping plans to a minimum means less disruption and frustration.

Some challenges may be more unavoidable such as the need to collect the children from school, appointments with the doctor, therapy sessions etc. Look for activities which reduce or eliminate stress levels and therefore reduce symptoms. Make room again for 'child whimsy'[216] such as painting, hobbies, creative writing, dog walking, play etc.

In summary; reintegrate into society and the workplace on your terms. Rather than feel you must do everything or confront and challenge every situation; choose your battles

---

[215] (Regel & Joseph, 2010)
[216] (Karpman, 1984)

and the ones worth succeeding in. We realised through trial and error that trying to tackle several challenges in the same week or the same day; resulted in exacerbated symptoms and exhaustion. Therefore we decided to focus on only one activity out of the house per day at most. Sometimes once a week was sufficient.

Social integration

One of the main difficulties stepping outside your front door is that you never know what stupidity or ignorance will cross your path, what immoral activity will take place in your line of sight, how other road users will behave and whose actions may put you or your family at risk. You will meet people who share your manners and attitudes and those who do not.

One of the important conversations my husband and I have had is around his new found freedom to associate with those he chooses to connect with. His role has been to deal with members of the public who (most often) operate from a very different set of values, morals and activities.

Moving away from the Police service allowed him to begin creating his own environment and surround himself with like-minded individuals who shared his interests and hobbies and provided him with positive encouragement and support. He found his hobby completely eliminated his flashbacks and kept him calm and relaxed; at least for the time he was involved in the activity.

He also expressed a desire to attend church and began to develop an interest in spirituality prior to his stress breakdown. He acknowledged that it was the promise of becoming part of a community who shared his morals and ethics, would do him no harm and a hope of 'belonging' which was the draw; more so than a connection with God.

Despite his feelings towards people in general and the difficulties he faces; he felt he wanted to 'give something back'. After serving his community and putting himself in dangerous situations on their behalf for 19 years; it cannot be said he has not already 'given' to others. However; working as a Police Officer does not necessarily induce gratitude and appreciation from community members. Helping people in ways which bring personal satisfaction and a sense of 'making a difference' is a whole other experience.

Family and friends may not understand your need to delay contact until a time when you feel able to talk. It is helpful to explain to them and your employer if you can; that going off the radar is a consequence of the PTS and you need them to respect your choice to not be constantly available. Whatever source of community and social interaction you choose to connect with; the most important point to remember is that *"there is overwhelming evidence that has shown that social support is a major protective factor following exposure to traumatic events or significant life crises."* (Regel & Joseph, 2010:42). PTS can sever our connections with others and the wider community.

"Trauma isolates; the group re-creates a sense of belonging...it is the strongest protection against ...despair [and] the strongest antidote to traumatic experience." (Herman, 1997:214)

Disclosure

Once you become consciously aware you are experiencing PTS you will make decisions whether to tell anyone and who to confide in. Depending on your relationships with your partner, family, friends, colleagues and your employer; this may present some difficulties or worries for you. Admitting you are affected by PTS, mental ill health or disability is the first step.

You may fear people's reactions to you, stigmatization, job security and concerns about your own self-image. Feelings of guilt and shame may inhibit your decision to share and disclose. You are the best person to know who you feel comfortable to talk to; particularly when you first make a disclosure. It is advisable to seek help as soon as you feel able. Early intervention can lessen the impact of symptoms and reduce risk. Speak to your GP about your symptoms and be as honest and open as you can. This will help your GP to make the most appropriate referrals for you.

Social support is incredibly important. The people living with you, close family and friends can help on a practical and emotional level. One possible reason for relationship breakdown is a lack of understanding between two people. The individual can present as someone who is dissatisfied in the relationship, withdrawn and disinterested in addition to other symptoms which can become difficult to live alongside. My husband needed permission to open up and disclose troubles kept in for years and to show his vulnerability. He felt it was a weakness. He had always been strong for us and protective. He felt he was letting us down. What he wanted most was validation. I said out loud 'I give you permission' and he broke down in tears. He had never cried before.

Sharing your thoughts and feelings with your partner and explaining what you are experiencing creates an opportunity for understanding and getting the support you need. This is also true of friends and family. Keeping everything bottled up and trying to hide the difficulties takes a great deal of energy and can add to stress, anxiety and exhaustion.

How can family and friends help?

You are likely to have people around you who want to help and can take off some of life's pressures; at least for a time, while you rest and recover. At a time when you are vulnerable and exhausted; it is advisable to get some help.[217]

---

[217] (Regel & Joseph, 2010)

Think about ways people can support you. What do you need? What are their individual strengths or interests? You can ask people to help you in specific ways or you can wait to see what support they offer.

Some ways people can help are:-
- ❖ Researching and sourcing information on PTSD, Welfare benefits, legal advice etc.
- ❖ Form filling
- ❖ Preparing freezer meals
- ❖ Activities together which give you a break from the symptoms, i.e. hobbies, relaxation, exercise
- ❖ A listening ear which is non-judgmental
- ❖ Housework and chores
- ❖ Phone calls, booking doctor appointments, dealing with household management etc.
- ❖ Doing the school run
- ❖ Having the children stay for a sleep over and giving you a good break
- ❖ Food shopping
- ❖ Walking the dog

Be careful not to have expectations of family and friends. They can only do what they feel able or comfortable to do. Even small gestures of support are welcome. Some will be more eager and willing to roll up their sleeves and help than others and that's okay. Some family and friends may take time to adjust to the situation and work out what they can offer. Give them time and they will likely come forward when they are ready. Sometimes people can be daunted by the notion of mental ill health, what is the best way to help, is this too big to deal with? And I'm not trained for this! Reassure family and friends that they are a huge help when they take on some of your normal, everyday jobs. Mum cooked us some meals to freeze.

We were both exhausted and at times had depression. It was a struggle to cook for the kids. It was such a great help. Family visited so my husband was not isolated.

Animal therapy
Animals can greatly support the individual with PTS. They are excellent companions because:-
- They love you unconditionally
- They can reduce stress and anger levels quickly and dogs in particular, will pick up on cues faster than family members or you
- Their needs are simple and they make little demands on you
- You can tell them your secrets, confessions, thoughts and feelings and they will not tell a soul
- Looking after animals can bring great satisfaction and purpose
- They are not concerned with petty moans and groans
- They are a source of joy, curiosity and entertainment
- They are trustworthy, will not screw you over to get ahead or use trickery and deception. They are an open book.
- Dogs can aid your restful sleep; knowing they will alert you to any dangers.

We had our dogs a couple of years before my husband became severely affected by PTSD. It became clear early on that the dogs were invaluable in reducing his stress and anger. Joe in particular was tuned in to changes in tone of voice and escalation in volume, as well as general mood changes. Where there was escalation; he would sit in front of Robert and draw attention to himself. He would go up on his hind legs and put his front paws on him and gently bark or he would tentatively nuzzle Robert.

Robert would immediately melt when he looked at him and you could see the anger dissipate instantly. He became more concerned with reassuring and calming Joe. This was a reaction I could not elicit myself (not that I have tried the same tactics!). Misty is less tuned in to mood changes but gives excellent cuddles and loves nothing more than curling up on his lap; providing an opportunity to calm and soothe whilst being stroked. On the rare occasion that he was particularly angry; there was little or no escalation, explosiveness or silent seething; they had the sense to disappear. I was always slower to cotton on. It is fair to say they prevented him taking his own life on more than one occasion; not because they were superheroes like Lassie; rather, they filled him with joy at his lowest moments; beckoning him back from despair with antics, playfulness and the validation that all he really needs is the simple things in life; because that's all they want and are quite happy. Perhaps their lifestyle strikes a chord with the individual with PTS who too is less preoccupied with the 'trappings' of culture, society, expectation and material considerations.

Dogs help with socialization. You find yourself approaching other dog walkers and striking up conversation. Chat is usually centred on the dogs and how cheeky Fido is or what naughty escapade he's been up to. Topics of discussion are safe and non-threatening and based on a shared interest and appreciation for dogs.

The U.S. are running programmes for veterans using Dog training to alleviate PTSD symptoms and improve quality of life.[218] Projects providing assistance dogs for Psychological disability in the UK are starting to develop.[219]

Self-assessment of Risk and Safety Plan

There are things you can do to reduce risk of harm to you and your family and we will look at some ideas for how to

---

[218] (Paws for Purple Hearts)
[219] (Psychological Assistance Dogs UK)

do this here. It is advisable to seek professional help, advice and support where possible.

Anger – Anger and rage can result in violence and will likely be followed by feelings of guilt and shame. Think about times when you have felt anger and rage, are you aware of the trigger? How did you react? Did you use any safety or coping strategies? How can your family help you? Learning coping strategies is the goal. However; if there is real and imminent risk of harm to anyone it is better to adopt a safety strategy, such as removing yourself from the situation and going to another room until you feel calmer.

In my opinion it is important to discuss this issue with your family. They can play an instrumental role in helping you and acting in ways which keep them safe. Discuss warning signs and triggers with them. Do they notice early signals that you are becoming agitated? For example, breathing rate, body language or tone of voice. Perhaps you drum and tap your fingers in impatience, your face hardens, you raise your voice or you hold your head in your hands whilst taking shallow breaths.

Speak to your GP about medication which can help with anxiety and anger. Robert found that his anger had difficulty escalating with the use of medication.

Explain to children in an age appropriate way that they can help through cooperation. Encourage them to resolve squabbles quickly and come up with solutions. Smaller children can be distracted by family members, taking them away from the situation or overcome tantrums more rapidly. Sometimes it may be necessary for the children to spend quiet time, playing calm quiet games or watching a movie. Noise, arguments and the potential for accidents, can be a factor for escalating anxiety.

Any issues which need to be discussed between partners or any disagreements which arise should be deferred to a time when the individual is calm and ready to have these conversations. This may mean prioritising the need to keep the environment calm and safe rather than meeting the immediate desire to 'get an answer' or a resolution. It is also advisable to not pursue the individual who is trying to remove themselves from the situation by walking out. Remember this is because your partner wants to safeguard you and following them around the house determined to finish the argument or debate, puts both of you at risk.

The individual must respect the needs of family members and not use 'time out' as a means to avoid difficult conversations. You should find a way to resume discussions when things have calmed down.

Self-harm or suicide

Self-harm can take many forms. It is any activity undertaken by the individual which is harmful to them. For example, substance or alcohol misuse, physical harm or sexual promiscuity. The individual may have thoughts of taking their own life, plan, attempt or carry it through. Factors which will most likely impact on self-harm and suicide either positively or negatively are:-

- ❖ Support networks, including friends, colleagues, groups, religious community, support agencies etc.
- ❖ Health care provision and support, including GP, mental health team, psychology services etc.
- ❖ Family relationships, particularly the strength and quality of relationship with partner, wider family support and any problems within the family, including perceived threats to loved ones, ill health or loss.
- ❖ Employer support, empathy, professionalism, sensitivity and understanding of mental ill health.
- ❖ Personality, temperament, character, including morals, ethics, principles, code of conduct, religious or spiritual beliefs, value system, family history of mental ill health.
- ❖ Symptoms of PTS, their intensity and longevity, including severity of flashbacks, anxiety and anger.

These factors will impact on all other areas of life for the individual too. The greater the support, empathy, understanding, help and responsiveness of everyone, the less hopeless the individual feels and the greater the validation of thoughts and feelings; resulting in better self-esteem and reducing the risk of self-loathing.

The PTSD sufferer is affected by thoughts and feelings relating to traumatic events, guilt over what they could have done better or different and perhaps a generalized kind of horror relating to what is witnessed and being plagued by repeated visions of these scenes. In addition; the individual may have thoughts and feelings of self-loathing when they no longer see themselves as useful, functional, supportive, protective or purposeful during a period of vulnerability, stress breakdown and beyond. Therefore; it is important to find ways to reduce symptoms positively using as many support networks as possible.

The individual can have suicidal thoughts on a daily basis or periodically. A need to be rid of flashbacks, intrusive memories, exhaustion and feelings of failure can incite suicide or thoughts of suicide. Robert identified that boredom and the need for risk had an impact on suicidal thoughts, as well as curiosity about what would happen. He acknowledges suicide or planning suicide has a strong link to a high risk situation. Suicide could be the ultimate adrenaline rush and the ultimate test. Throughout years of high stakes situations and dalliance with fate; the individual goads fate in turn.

On the edge of life and death

The following, is one representation of total despair and being on the edge of life and death, with excerpts from Carl Jung's' Memories, Dreams, Reflections (1995).

It began with feeling trapped in an emotional and mental hell, with no relent. Then there was the numbing of the senses. Dullness filled the heart and mind and every movement of the body appeared slow and light. *[In an utterly transformed state... I felt as though I were floating in space... safe in the womb of the universe-Carl Jung]*

A new reality came into vision; one more real than this. The old world dimmed and I saw it for what it was; a falsehood. *[behind the horizon of the cosmos a three dimensional world had been artificially built up… Carl Jung]*

It felt like the most natural act; to fall silently and softly and disappear into the earth as dust. There was no fear of pain, no fear of hell or anticipation of heaven; just a comforting feeling of love, care and acceptance. *[neither joyful or sad, but, rather objectively wise and understanding without the slightest emotional reaction... beyond the mists of affects – Carl Jung]*

I clung to my existence for the sake of my family. I struggled to bring my mind back to the physical world of 'matter'. I had become aware of the fringes of another dimension. It was difficult to psychologically re-connect with life on earth, its trivia and pointlessness.

['..and now I should have to convince myself all over again that this was important! Life and the whole world struck me as a prison'…….
'..in reality, a good three weeks were still to pass before I could truly make up my mind to live again…' – Carl Jung]

Criminal offence

The individual with PTS is at risk of committing a criminal offence in relation to:-

- ❖ Alcohol misuse resulting in 'drunk and disorderly' or drink driving offences etc.
- ❖ Domestic violence
- ❖ Public order offences, such as affray.
- ❖ Common assault, actual bodily harm, grievous bodily harm etc.
- ❖ Possession of illegal substances
- ❖ Alcohol use can result in driving over the legal limit and increasing the likelihood of violence or aggression and public disorder.

❖ Outbursts of rage and anger can result in violence towards family members or anyone 'in the wrong place at the wrong time'.

Think about agencies or trusted people who you feel comfortable to speak to about any of these issues, get support and come up with a management plan.

I kept self-incarcerated at home. I had anxiety about going out. I came to realize I wasn't afraid of everyone else out there and what they could do to me; I was afraid of the harm I could do to other people – Robert

Risk Safety Plan

You are likely to get a mixed response from support agencies, healthcare agencies, employer, friends and family. Some support will be better and more forthcoming or expeditious than others. Therefore, some degree of self-efficacy is advisable; particularly while you are waiting for support or healthcare. However; this can be no replacement for professional support and advice.

Robert was told there was a two year waiting list for psychology support (for urgent cases). Fortunately, he started his treatment 7 months after referral. He chose not to continue; believing CBT could not undo the 'moral injury' and he had the ability to develop his own coping strategies. He believes his best resources are good quality sleep, medication, family, friends and acceptance of his situation and how his life has altered.

Robert had to research support agencies for himself and agree a strategy for living with PTS in collaboration with his family. Without self-efficacy supported heavily by his partner; the risk of suicide and hopelessness was a clear and present danger.

Duty of Care

I have included a simple risk assessment form here which you may find of use for organising your thoughts, agreeing an action plan and for reference as and when needed. The idea is that you make decisions about what actions to take to reduce the risk you identify. The completed form here is based on the risk of 'anger, rage and short temper'. You could also use it for self-harm, suicide, financial loss or hardship, housing issues, returning to work and any other area you wish to explore. Decide which actions may reduce the risk from high to medium etc.

What is the identified risk?	Who is at risk?	What is the potential impact on those at risk?
Short temper, anger, rage	Me, my partner, my children, the public	Physical assault, criminal conviction, hospitalization

Is the risk of harm or injury perceived to be:-

NOT IMMINENT (L) ☐
LIKELY IN THE NEAR FUTURE (M) ☐
LIKELY IN THE IMMEDIATE FUTURE (H) ✓
(Low-L) (Moderate-M) (High-H)

STRATEGIES TO REDUCE RISK	In Place Y/N	Notes
Explore warning signs and triggers with family members	Y	
Remove myself from the situation and go to another room etc.	Y	
Explore ways family can help	Y	Quiet playtime, cooperation
Speak to the GP about therapies and medication	Y	
Seek support from local agencies, such as 'Mind'	Y	
Risk score after measures in place (L/M/H)?	**M**	

A note on Disability

Post-Traumatic Stress can go undetected in the serving Police Officer for years. The Officer will most likely have adapted to the symptoms over time and developed coping strategies and safety strategies which become normality.

The Officer, family members, colleagues and line managers may not have identified the Post-Traumatic Stress, despite some signs and symptoms of stress being exhibited.

Therefore; an Officer can live with Post-Traumatic Stress and continue to function 'normally' on a day to day basis. Post-Traumatic Stress can become a disability when 'normal' day to day functioning is significantly impaired.

The Equality Act (EqA) explains the definition of disability and 'normal' day to day functioning in more detail.[220] It is not the label or diagnosis of Post-Traumatic Stress Disorder which determines disability. The act defines disability based on the individuals' day to day functioning, difficulties experienced and long term effects.[221]

Two people with a diagnosis of PTSD, Depression or Anxiety (for example) can be affected differently and to a lesser or greater degree. Therefore it is not the diagnosis but the effects on the individual which are considered.[222] An individual can be treated for symptoms and given a prognosis for recovery regardless of whether there is a diagnosis. Not everyone will want a formal diagnosis (or label) and this must be respected.

---

[220] (Equality Act 2010 Guidance; Guidance On Matters To Be Taken Into Account In Determining Questions Relating To The Definition Of Disability, 2011)

[221] (Lewis T. , 2011)

[222] (Lewis T. , 2011)

For some; a diagnosis can mean validation and being believed. It can assist with explaining the situation to family and friends and sourcing further reading and information on the subject.

An employer has a duty to make adjustments when they can reasonably be expected to know or they do know that a person may have a disability[223] regardless of whether or not there has been a 'formal' diagnosis. They also need to be clear what constitutes a 'formal diagnosis' for the purposes of identifying disability.

A person has a disability for the purposes of the Act if he or she has a physical or mental impairment and the impairment has a substantial and long-term adverse effect on his or her ability to carry out normal day-to-day activities (S6(1))... which has lasted at least 12 months; or where the total period for which it lasts, from the time of the first onset, is likely to be at least 12 months; or which is likely to last for the rest of the life of the person affected- (Equality Act 2010 guidance)

A diagnosis from a GP or CPN is acceptable. A diagnosis of Depression may qualify as a disability if it meets the definition of the EqA. Furthermore; as your employer they have a responsibility under legislation to explore how you are affected by your ill health and support you with reasonable adjustments[224] to the workplace, your role and procedures; including during sickness absence.

The Disability Discrimination Act 1995 (DDA) was incorporated into the Equality Act 2010 (EqA). Cases of discrimination under the DDA only applies to those before 1st October 2010.

---

[223] (Employment Statutory Code of Practice, 2011)
[224] (Employment Statutory Code of Practice, 2011)

Duty of Care

Your employer should be working from the EqA and disregard the previously used list for defining disability[225] which was:-

At least one of these areas must be severely affected:
- Mobility
- Manual dexterity
- Physical co-ordination
- Continence
- Ability to lift, carry or move everyday items
- Speech, hearing or eyesight
- Memory or ability to concentrate, learn or understand.

Robert was on sickness absence for 16 months. He provided GP certificates for depression and work related stress, a CPN letter with a diagnosis of PTSD and an FMA (Force Medical Advisor) report with a diagnosis of PTSD which outlined problems with day to day functioning. Robert told his employer he considered himself to have a disability.

Robert was told by his employer that they would not acknowledge he had a disability until he had a formal diagnosis from a psychologist or psychiatrist and therefore did not assess him for disability, did not make adjustments or allowances for him during his sickness absence, would not accept it was a workplace injury, labelled him as uncooperative and rejected his appeal against a reduction in pay.

If you feel you have been discriminated against by your employer in relation to disability; it is advisable to seek legal advice through an employment lawyer. You may get funding for this through an insurance scheme. 'Mind' has legal advice available and you can find information via their website. ACAS have a helpline number and advice online.

---

[225] (Lewis T. , 2011)

The rules on applications to Employment Tribunal changed from 6th May 2014 and ACAS are to manage early conciliation. If the two parties cannot agree on conciliation then the case may be eligible for Employment Tribunal. Matters of public interest or 'whistleblowing' can go to Tribunal without first going through conciliation.[226]

The new Code of Ethics states *"The policing profession will protect whistle blowers according to the law"* and asks colleagues to report unethical or unprofessional behaviour regardless of the person's rank or role.[227] It is anticipated that Officers will be able to hold supervisory ranks and civilian staff accountable for failing to take complaints seriously and take appropriate action. The following types of disability discrimination are:-[228]

Direct discrimination is where the employer treats the individual less favourably based on his/her disability

Indirect discrimination is where a provision, criterion or practice which appears neutral (treats everyone the same), disadvantages the individual with a 'protected characteristic'

Harassment occurs when the individual is subjected to conduct which violates their dignity or creates an intimidating, hostile, degrading, humiliating or offensive work environment.

Victimization occurs when the employer punishes the individual because s/he has made a complaint or grievance about discrimination.

---

[226] (Early Conciliation)
[227] (Code of Ethics, 2014)
[228] (Lewis T. , 2008) (Disability discrimination - legal briefing)

Failure to make reasonable adjustments occurs when the employer puts the individual at a disadvantage in the workplace, because nothing is done to remedy the disadvantage resulting from an effect of the disability by way of reasonable adjustments to the environment or procedures etc.

Discrimination arising from disability occurs when the individual is treated unfavourably due to something happening as a consequence of their disability, such as a behaviour or an incapacity.[229]

Encouraging others to discriminate is also considered by a tribunal.

---

[229] (Lewis T. , 2011)

8 CARERS & FAMILY

Fears and anxieties can be passed on to close family members through Compassion Fatigue. Trauma can be contagious.[230] Close family and friends can develop PTS symptoms as a result of supporting and caring for their loved one.[231] Here are some symptoms which may be experienced by those living with the individual who is affected by PTS.

Partners and close family members may experience:-
- Nervous anxiety when out and about
- Scanning for possible triggers to your partners anxiety, anger and distress
- Hyper-vigilant to changes in the individuals mood, facial expression and body language
- Feeling numb or empty
- Fearfulness
- Withdrawal from social networks, family and friends

---

[230] (Herman, 1997) (Salston & Figley, 2003)
[231] (Salston & Figley, 2003)

- ❖ Isolation
- ❖ Rage or anger disproportionate to the situation
- ❖ Emotional stress experienced as physical illness, such as stomach cramps, muscle tension, headaches, migraines, colds and flu etc.
- ❖ Degree of depression
- ❖ Feelings of guilt
- ❖ Tearfulness
- ❖ Exhaustion, tiredness and lethargy
- ❖ Difficulty trusting others
- ❖ Confusion or forgetfulness
- ❖ Compulsive behaviour
- ❖ Separation/ relationship breakdown

Possible reasons for becoming vigilant to your partners' mood or triggers in the environment may be the need to protect yourself and your children from harm; potentially serious physical harm. If your partner's behaviour is unpredictable, explosive or unstable, it makes sense that you will naturally develop your own behaviour and instinct around threat. The degree at which you experience vigilance is likely to depend on your personal circumstances, your relationship, what incidents have occurred before and the presence or absence of domestic violence.

If your partner has begun to withdraw affection and/or intimacy; this can leave you feeling rejected and unloved and if these needs in the relationship are not met or discussed; it can lead to a couple drifting apart or possibly separating.

It is important to understand your partner is not withholding affection. S/he may feel unable to demonstrate closeness due to a consequence of the post-traumatic stress. The development of emotional numbing occurs to adjust to dealing with distressing work related incidents. It may also be strengthened by upsetting personal events; such as bereavement. In addition; your partner is likely to be affected by physical exhaustion as a consequence of persistent physiological hyper-arousal; such as preparing for fight or flight response, exerting physical energy in keeping anger under control, lack of sleep or disturbed sleep patterns and contending with flashbacks.

Your partner may have some degree of depression and low self-esteem. You may feel guilty for complaining about the impact of your partner's PTS on you personally; given the nature of Police work, the traumatic events your partner has dealt with and any debilitating consequences of PTS. However; it is important to acknowledge the effect on you, your relationship and your family.

Caring for your partner and any children, adjusting to their new disability, advocating for them and how they are treated, home management, mental anguish over the future and 'suicide watch' can become exhausting.

When you break it all down; there is a great deal of work to do and emotions to manage. It can all take its toll on you and you can find yourself drained of energy, tearful and depressed.

Caring for your partner under these circumstances is a commitment and you may or may not feel obligated to stay in the relationship. Making decisions about your relationship may depend on:-

- ❖ The quality of feeling in the relationship prior to PTS
- ❖ Whether the relationship is primarily based on friendship or other solid connection
- ❖ The risks to you and your children
- ❖ Whether your future aspirations, career or social life are unacceptably jeopardized.
- ❖ The quality of feeling in the relationship following PTS

It may be necessary to separate for a time whilst your partner makes a degree of recovery which reduces the risk of harm to you and your children.

You will need to make your own assessment of the likelihood and impact of harm. I have included a risk assessment document on P.150 which may help you to organize your thoughts and agree any actions you need to take.

If you experience domestic violence or abuse; you can approach your local council about temporary accommodation; including refuge or safe house. You may have the option of moving in with family or it may be that your partner finds alternative accommodation. However; be mindful that your partner is potentially very vulnerable. It is important for everyone involved to balance risk to them.

Your partner may think about leaving in the interests of safety and it is important for both of you to treat this decision with respect. If your partner believes there is a significant risk of harm to his or her family; this can bring great anxiety and further stress. Causing harm to loved ones, without the intention to do so will cause further psychological injury.

It is important not to use 'PTSD' as a means to prohibit child contact. Parent and child relationships are important to both parties. Find ways to safely maintain these relationships. If everyone lives together; think about what each person can do to reduce risk in the home. If you are separated; think about which environments are the most conducive to safe contact, including who should be present. If you need help with this; think about getting advice and support.

The risk of suicide

If your partner has thoughts of or plans out suicide; it can be a very worrying time. I prevented my husband from taking his own life on two occasions. Both times; an inner voice told me I needed to check on him and that he wasn't okay.

During this time, it was obvious he was struggling and feeling trapped by unresolved conflicts with his employer.

There have been other times when he has thought about it and I was none the wiser. I thought he was getting better. He told me days or weeks after, that he had been thinking about suicide again. This was harder to cope with for me, because I had allowed myself to let my guard down and had become complacent. I felt these moments were the most dangerous. I will never know if a day will come when he takes this step.

This is a difficult subject to broach because we hold ethical, moral, cultural and religious beliefs around suicide. The only advice I can offer from a personal perspective is that the individual will always find a way to take their own life if it is their intention to do so. Rather than live in fear, guilt and bear responsibility for what may or may not happen; you can remain supportive, non-judgmental, watchful and respectful. Living with the horror of PTSD when the symptoms are potent and all-consuming is a relentless torment..

I had always been anti-suicide and felt there is always something to live for. Now I know what it is like to feel suicidal and what can bring you to this point. It has brought me greater understanding of people and that you should never judge someone else. You have to walk in their shoes before you can understand – (Robert)

Talking to children about PTS

How you raise the issue of PTS with your child will depend on your own personal circumstances and the character of the individual child. I wanted to include some ideas and suggestions for doing this in the book because it can be a tricky subject to tackle and not discussing Mum or Dad's behaviour could result in the child internalizing powerful emotions and self-blame.

Remember that behaviour in the parent can be confusing to the child; rules, boundaries and discipline can become erratic or inconsistent and the child may feel responsible for angry or violent episodes or mood swings in the parent.

It is important to encourage understanding without justifying negative behaviour as excusable or acceptable. Although PTS can be seen as a consequence of heroism; it is perhaps unwise to explain Mum or Dad behaves this way because they had to deal with terrible things and they were so brave; they're a hero. I would be concerned that this message would become embedded and result in the adult-child perceiving an abusive or violent relationship as acceptable, the relationship would be based on sympathy and feeling duty bound or obligated to stay in a relationship which is unhealthy.

We agreed to sit the older children down and speak to them about recent events because trying to keep it a secret and 'protect' them from what was happening was putting incredible stress on us and we felt it important to explain to them why he was off work, why he had had some angry outbursts and why he sometimes went off to be alone. We realized we were not protecting them by 'keeping a lid' on things. We enabled them to play an active role in supporting the family unit, learn self-discipline, autonomy and responsibility.

This is not to say they became carers or took on adult responsibilities and this is an important distinction to make. The children were asked to be responsible for themselves and their own behaviour in an age appropriate way. They were asked to develop a level of maturity which was fitting for a 12 and 15 year old.

This didn't happen overnight with the wave a wand and I would like to reassure parents everywhere that it is an ongoing project and I have no miracle solution for getting children to co-operate or stop siblings bickering over trivial matters. This leads me to say that it is also important to allow children to develop naturally, express their own emotion and learn to interact, socialize and co-operate with others as a matter of course. Subservience and control through fear must be avoided. This course of action is unhealthy and damaging for the child and will impact on the child well into adulthood and possibly throughout their life.

My husband explained that he had been affected by some experiences at work which were unpleasant. Our 12 year old said in a matter-of-fact manner; "what-like seeing dead bodies?" to which he said yes and explained there had been other things too. He told them there may be times when he needed to go off and be alone or there may be times when he gets really angry.

He made it clear to the children that it wasn't because they had done anything wrong. The kids responded with "it's okay"; which is the usual response from most kids when they either don't know what else to say or want to make their parents feel better. He said "it's not okay. It's not acceptable. I wanted you to know it's not your fault if I behave this way. It's my responsibility". He also explained that he gets flashbacks and remembers what happened like a nightmare.

I started teaching the children the signs when their Dad was feeling unwell, struggling to cope with flashbacks or trying to stay calm. I would be the first to notice when he was in difficulty and quietly drew the children's attention to their Dad; usually followed by a finger to my lips (asking them to reduce the noise level), draw my finger round my face in a circle (asking them to notice their Dad's face) or I would simply say "kids, your Dads not feeling well". Most often; this was all that needed to be said and the kids responded immediately.

They didn't run for the hills or become anxious or scared. They're response was more nonchalant. They demonstrated understanding of what was required. They didn't ignore him or isolate him; rather they gave him some space; perhaps make everyone a cup of tea and relaxed around him or found things to occupy themselves.

It is empowering and confidence building for children to know and feel they have the ability to influence their environment and others in positive ways; that they have power and control of their own. Useful information on this topic can be found online at www.ptsd.va.gov. In particular; the article 'when a child's parent has PTSD' (Price, 2014).

Domestic Violence and abuse in the context of PTS

Domestic abuse in general terms is when one person in the relationship purposefully uses behaviour to control the other. The behaviour is extreme and persistent. It results in making the other person subservient and dependent, isolates them and inhibits them intentionally. Most organisations working in this field believe domestic abuse is the result of an imbalance of power between men and women, based on gender specific roles, inequality in those roles and how men view women and their worth.

Domestic violence and abuse can affect people regardless of gender or sexuality. It may or may not be present in a relationship affected by PTS. It is important to make the distinction that violence in the home may be the result of symptoms and brain functioning rather than the intention to assert control over another person.

However; there may be some cross-over in the type of behaviour demonstrated by someone suffering from PTS and someone experiencing domestic abuse, such as:-

❖ Withdrawal and disinterestedness, resulting in isolation from family and friends

- ❖ Withholding affection or intimacy
- ❖ Unpredictable outbursts resulting in walking on egg shells and not knowing what the rules are
- ❖ Alcohol or substance misuse
- ❖ Unpredictable violence.
- ❖ Rapid escalation in anger and outburst
- ❖ Violence towards children

It is not necessarily that domestic abuse is present in the context of its widely accepted and general definition and includes verbal, emotional, sexual, financial or physical abuse as a means of having power and control over another person.

Behaviours are a consequence of PTS and adaptation to stressful environments; resulting in an impact on family members living alongside these behaviours.

"Although PTSD is associated with increased risk of violence, the majority of people with PTSD have no history of violent behavior", *"Individuals with PTSD are not dangerous"* (Norman et al., 2014)

Other factors specific to the individual should be taken into consideration when assessing risk; such as other psychiatric disorders, substance or alcohol misuse etc.[232]

We also explored 'authoritarianism' in Police Culture which can affect home life too. Very often an authoritative stance towards family members is because the individual fears for their safety and has anxiety about the dangers they may be exposed to.

If you feel it is unsafe to stay in the relationship; seek advice from agencies who can help. Bear in mind that these agencies are most likely to come from a feminist and orthodox perspective on domestic abuse and may not

---

[232] (Norman, Elbogen, & Schnurr, 2014)

understand PTSD. However; you can get advice on refuge accommodation, outreach support, welfare benefits and housing etc. (there are projects available regardless of gender or sexuality) across the UK; though the greater majority are for women or women with children.

9 SUPPORT, ADVICE & FINANCIAL HELP

Long term sickness and retirement can be a worrying time financially. There is probably more support and assistance available than you realize. It can be difficult taking the step of benefit applications, though it may become necessary.

We were pleasantly surprised and are excessively grateful to the benefit agencies for our own experience of the welfare system. Not least of all for the non-judgmental and supportive attitude of the call-takers and the efficiency at which our claims were handled and processed.

Roberts' Statutory Sick Pay ended and he applied for ESA (Employment Support Allowance), his pay was cut by half. Fortunately, he had an insurance policy to cover sickness and redundancy and he was able to get his wages topped up through this each month. It is important to note that the federation group insurance does not top you up to full pay (as is popular belief) or certainly not in all force areas.

Benefits change periodically and so it is best to get the most up to date information on benefits from the relevant agencies. Speak to the DWP (Department for Work and Pensions), for information about making a claim. Once statutory sick pay comes to an end (after 26 weeks); you will need to apply for ESA which has replaced incapacity benefit. Your employer should advise you to do this at the appropriate time and provide you with the necessary information. ESA is often used as qualifying criteria for other benefits.

Some of the main benefits to explore are:-
ESA
Child Tax Credit
Free school meals (dependent on qualifying benefits or income)
Council tax benefit (dependent on household income)
Housing Benefit (rented accommodation)
SMI (support for Mortgage interest – income related benefit)
Disability benefit
Industrial Injuries Disablement Benefit

The benefits advisor will be able to tell you what benefits you may be entitled to, based on the information you provide about your circumstances and household income.

I would expect any Officer on long term sickness absence with a workplace injury (including psychological) to be in receipt of full pay and not need to apply for benefits. Certainly; the Chief Constable is advised to do so. In Roberts' case, appeal against half pay was rejected and his appeal against nil pay resulted in continuance on half pay (reviewed every month, subject to reports etc.). Full pay was reinstated whilst going through the EIHR process.

Financial constraints can add to isolation. SMI benefit can prevent homelessness and enable you to stay in your own home. Interest on our mortgage may be covered by this benefit and paid direct to your lender. Your mortgage lender is obligated to prevent homelessness as far as possible and it is advisable to speak to them as soon as you think you may have difficulties. The lender can have conversations with you about how they may be able to assist.

Speak to a financial advisor to discuss how to get the most out of your money, benefits available, mortgage products and options for maximizing your commutation and income.

If you pay into an Insurance scheme you may be able to make a claim. If you pay into the Federation group insurance you will need to check the policy for your force area as each force negotiates its' own package. Perhaps the most useful insurance policies to have are legal cover (which may be included in one of your existing policies – such as home insurance), private health insurance which includes treatment for mental ill health (which is not chronic) and Personal Protection Plan to include life cover, critical illness cover, income/sickness cover or mortgage/rent cover and permanent total disablement cover (occupational). It is important to highlight that there are different types of permanent total disablement cover and some are more restrictive than others. Occupational cover will usually provide you with a financial award if you are no longer able to carry out your usual occupation due to permanent disablement (including psychological). If you were to take EIHR for this reason; you could be entitled to an insurance claim. Seek professional financial advice on insurance policies.

Remember you may be entitled to an Injury on duty award via your Constabulary. Make an application via your HR department if this appropriate.

Industrial injury disablement benefit is available through application to the DWP if you qualify. They are familiar with applications from blue light services. They require some detail of the incidents, such as the nature of the incidents and dates if possible. They determine how much you are entitled to from this information.

10 CONCLUSION & RECOMMENDATIONS

Risk factors involved in developing psychological injury, long term sickness absence, reduced efficiency and EIHR in Police Officers are:-
- ❖ The persistent nature of the job role; both extraordinary and routine
- ❖ Organizational considerations; including leadership, management, workload, expectations, 'moral injury', personnel systems, lack of autonomy or involvement in decisions and support provision.
- ❖ Community; both within the Police Force and the wider community
- ❖ Re-victimization and traumatization of the Officer
- ❖ Character and Temperament; including the 'Be strong driver' and the 'avoidant' personality, sense of mission, rescuer mentality and lack of boundaries or limitations.
- ❖ Police Culture
- ❖ Exposure to traumatic events, human degradation

and suffering
- ❖ Secondary Traumatic Stress, Vicarious Traumatization, Burnout and Compassion Fatigue
- ❖ Emotional Dissonance

Research into Police Culture, PTSD among Police Officers and other groups, the impact of organizational considerations on individuals and comparable psychological conditions, have come together in this book to produce a 'bigger picture' of PTS and indeed psychological health in the Police as a whole.

We have travelled far from initial understanding of PTSD. The belief it results from a single traumatic incident, is a sign of weakness and is an illness; has been quashed.

We have highlighted that Police Officers with PTS are human like everyone else and at the same time have more resilience, strength, belief in 'what's right', sense of mission, desire for justice and courage than most others. We all owe them a debt of gratitude for the challenges they face on our behalf and the sacrifices they make in the process, such as psychological and physical injury and the impact on their relationships with others.

We have discovered that dealing with psychological health in Policing cannot be as simplistic as offering counselling sessions after a significant traumatic event or after the Officer seeks support from Occupational Health. A proactive stance is preferable to the current reactive response and a variety of strategies for protecting Officers is available and must be implemented.

Discussion around character and temperament have raised the question about the 'kind' of Officer we want in service. Do we want Police Officers with a strong 'sense of mission' to protect and safeguard victims, empathy for people in the community who are suffering, strength of character to repeatedly 'get the job done' and push through difficulties because we expect it and demand it? Do we want Officers who are avoidant of types of work and situations? Can we create a work environment for characters to flourish? Can we adopt positive reinforcement instead of punitive tactics to draw out the avoidant person and allow them to feel safe to operate effectively; to reinforce pride and security in the Officer who puts themselves out in front, time after time? Can we change the culture of the strong silent type and create a safe environment to open up and talk or seek support? Can we encourage this person to explore their limitations through competent, supportive and strong leadership?

Is the Police Service ready and willing to make the necessary changes which will see Officers protected from psychological harm and buffered against the impact of everything the job throws their way?

We have learnt that the organisation is the single most significant factor in protection against long term psychological injury.[233] You probably thought nothing could be done; that dealing with trauma was a normal part of the job and therefore Psychological problems are inevitable? We now know there is much the organisation can do on a practical, every day basis through their personnel systems, Occupational Health and Welfare departments, Management and Leadership behaviour. 'Support' is not limited to a shoulder to cry on or 'fluffy, wooly stuff' such as talking therapies. Support has greater

---

[233] (Dobby, Anscombe, & Tuffin, 2004) (ACPO, 2012) (Bakker & Heuven, 2006) (Carlier, Lamberts, & Gersons, 1997) (Hayday, Broughton, & Tyers, 2007) (Maguen, Metzier, Inslicht, Henn-Haase, Neylan, & Marmar, 2009) (Management Of Stress At Work Policy, 2007) (Metcalfe & Dick, 2000) (Mitchell, Stevenson, & Poole, 2001) (Oliver & Meier, 2009) (Salston & Figley, 2003) (Shay, Achilles In Vietnam: Combat Trauma And The Undoing Of Character, 2003) (Shay, Odysseus In America: Combat Trauma And The Trials Of Homecoming, 2002)

diversity and comes in many varied forms.[234] Support is what the individual needs it to be.

In our experience, the Constabulary could not understand that 'doing things right', responsiveness to needs and communications, following policies, providing guidance on procedures, involving my husband in decisions about his welfare and sickness absence, treating him with dignity and respect, providing explanation when reasonable queries were raised and demonstrating integrity, honesty and openness were all forms of 'support' which were not provided.

Support should not end with the termination of employment. In the interests of recovery; the Officer needs to feel his/her efforts across their career have been recognized and valued. A perfunctory letter confirming termination of employment (EIHR) with no real acknowledgement of the injury on duty; raises the question of what was it all for. The Officer has become disposable, will not be remembered or missed. More effort must be invested in aiding psychological wellbeing at the point of retirement. It is recommended that a personal letter from the Chief Constable or community leaders is afforded Officers retired due to an injury on duty in recognition of their sacrifice and dedication to their community.

Effective support from the organisation is to be found in peers, leaders, education and regular supervision,[235] openness, honesty between ranks, good communication, feedback on performance, taking time to listen, desistance of blame, removal of command and control management systems, appropriate selection and promotion,[236] and managers demonstrating they are aware and empathetic of the difficulties faced by Bobbies.

---

[234] (Mitchell, Stevenson, & Poole, 2001)
[235] (Salston & Figley, 2003)
[236] (Metcalfe & Dick, 2000)

Responsibilities held by Constabularies

STOP	START
Using Blame	Taking responsibility and accountability
Applying authoritarian and directive management style to the Officers' personal issues	Providing Support and Welfare which is person centered and Officer led.
Discrepancy between how various ranks apply and utilize policies and procedures	Applying The Code of Ethics, Policies and Procedures equally across all ranks.
Inappropriate promotion and unfair selection processes	Career movements based on merit and demonstration of ability
Using abusive tactics of power and control	Using positive reinforcement and comradery to encourage greater commitment to the organisation and its' goals.
Using punitive measures as a reaction to events	Adopting a supportive and empathetic stance in the first instance and explore any problems or difficulties the Officer may have.
Threatening insubordination when Officers challenge misconduct assertively	Supporting Officers who stand up for 'what's right' in the workplace and ensuring 'what's right' is upheld.

Ignoring the existence of Psychological Injury	Educating Constabularies in all ranks and roles about the signs and symptoms and what they can do to assist others. Ensure new recruits and Officers are aware of the dangers and how individuals can take care of their mental health
Using deviant behaviour with colleagues which breeds distrust	Building rapport and trust with colleagues so that regular supervision and consultation with Officers is effective

Self-efficacy

The Officer can take steps to safeguard their psychological health by:-

- ❖ Avoiding the 'rescuer' mentality, know your limits and boundaries and make time for fun and pleasure.[237]
- ❖ Maintaining a healthy balanced diet and exercise routine.[238]
- ❖ Seeking regular supervision.[239] Consider private clinical supervision with a counsellor if you feel more comfortable with this.
- ❖ Avoiding isolation and withdrawal and invest in support networks outside of work which will help you cope; such as family, friends, interests and social activities[240]

---

[237] (Salston & Figley, 2003)
[238] (Salston & Figley, 2003)
[239] (Salston & Figley, 2003)
[240] (Salston & Figley, 2003)

- ❖ Aiming for acceptance of the changes you are experiencing rather than deny or minimize the effects.[241]
- ❖ Familiarizing yourself with the signs and symptoms[242] of psychological injury and seek early intervention.

---

[241] (Salston & Figley, 2003)
[242] (Salston & Figley, 2003)

Claire McDowall

Appendix 1

FOI Request – Thames Valley Police

7 May 2014

I write in connection with the above-referenced Freedom of Information Act (FOIA) request submitted on 8 April 2014. Thames Valley Police has now considered this request, which for clarity, has been repeated below:

Request
Please could you provide me with the following information; relating to each year between 2008-2013:-

How many Police Officers were referred for Psychological assessment?

Response
2008 – no information held, 2009 – 21, 2010 – 4, 2011 – 0, 2012 – 0, 2013 – 29

How many police officers were diagnosed with PTSD or Psychological injury?

No information is held. Thames Valley Police can confirm that the diagnoses are made and held by external medical practitioners.

How many police officers took Early ill health retirement due to PTSD or Psychological injury?

2008 – no information held, 2009 – no information held, 2010 – 9, 2011 – 1, 2012 – 7, 2013 - 1

Appendix 2

Birmingham & Solihull Mental Health NHS Foundation Trust

Response to FOI0109

Request:

Please could you tell me how many police officers have been referred to psychology and psychiatry services and the community mental health team for each year between 2008 and 2013?

Please could you tell me how many police officers have been diagnosed with PTSD for the same period?

Response:

Information not held because the Trust does not routinely collect the occupation of our service users in a reportable way.

Appendix 3

Home Office

25th March 2014

Reference 31006

Dear Claire

Thank you for your e-mail of 5 March 2014, in which you ask for information relating to all 43 police forces across the UK relating to sickness absence and ill health.
You requested the following information for the period 2003-2013 inclusive and a breakdown of information for each year during this period:-
Number of police officers (all ranks) who are recorded as taking sickness absence because of:-

PTSD, Post-Traumatic Stress Syndrome Work related stress, Anxiety, Depression, Occupational stress, Stress, Any other mental health disorder or illness

Number of police officers (all ranks) who committed suicide or employment was terminated because of death by suicide.

Number of police officers (all ranks) granted Early Ill Health Retirement (EIHR) on the grounds of mental ill health.

Number of police officers (all ranks) applied for and denied Early Ill Health Retirement on the grounds of mental ill health.

Number of police officers referred for psychiatric or psychological assessment by the police and the same for primary care?

Number of police officers receiving psychiatric or psychological treatment funded by the police and the same through the NHS?

Number of police officers referred for counselling through the police and the same for primary care?

Number of police officers referred for critical incident debrief by the police?

Number of police officers referred for CBT (cognitive behavioural therapy) by the police and the same for primary care?

Your request has been handled as a request for information under the Freedom of Information Act 2000. The Home Office does not hold the information which you requested for the 43 police forces of England and Wales. The Home Office collects data on the number of police officers on long-term absence broken down by absence type, including certified sickness. However, further breakdowns providing the reasons for certified sickness are not collected.

The Home Office also collects data on the number of police officer leavers broken down by reasons for leaving, including death. However, further breakdowns into the cause of death are not collected. The Home Office also collects data on the number of ill-health retirements. However, breakdowns providing the reasons for ill-health retirement are not collected. Figures for Scotland and Northern Ireland are a matter for the Devolved Administrations.

Appendix 4

Norfolk Constabulary

8th May 2014

Freedom of Information Request Reference No: FOI 18/14/15

I write in connection with your request for information received by the Norfolk Constabulary on the 8th April 2014 in which you sought access to the following information:

Please could you provide me with the following information; relating to each year between 2008-2013:-

How many police officers were referred for Psychological assessment?

How many police officers were diagnosed with PTSD or Psychological injury?

How many police officers took early ill health retirement due to PTSD or Psychological injury?

Response to your Request

When responding to a request for information under the terms of the Freedom of Information Act, a public authority is not obliged to provide information if the authority estimates that the cost of the retrieval of the information requested would be in excess of £450 (equivalent to 18 hours work).

The costs criteria relates to a request in its entirety, which means that if we cannot retrieve all of the information requested within the costs limit, we are not obliged to retrieve *any* of the information requested.

The Norfolk Constabulary estimates that to retrieve all the information you have requested would exceed cost in excess of £450.

In order to establish what information may be held, relevant to your request we have contacted our Human Resources Department. They have advised on the following:-

Information relevant to points 1 and 2 of your request is not centrally recorded. Referrals could be at the request of the officers General Practitioner, rather than the force medical advisor. It is at the individual's own discretion as to whether they inform the Force of any referral / diagnosis made by their personal GP. Any information which might be held would be recorded within an Officers personnel file. As at 30.04.14 the Constabulary had 1,608 officers and it is estimated that it would take 30 minutes per officer file to manually search for the information you have requested. This would equate to approximately 804 hours to complete.

With regards to point 3 of your request, from 01.04.2008 to 31.3.2014 I can advise that there were 43 Ill Health Retirements. As above each personnel file would need to be looked at to see whether the retirement was due to PTSD or Psychological injury. Again, estimating at 30 minutes per file, this would equate to 21.5 hours

This would exceed the appropriate limit for dealing with a Freedom of Information request, in terms of costs, and therefore Section 12(1) of the Freedom of Information Act applies.

Section 12(1) of the Freedom of Information Act states that a public authority is not obliged to:

"...comply with a request for information if the authority estimates that the cost of complying with the request would exceed the appropriate limit".

The Freedom of Information (Appropriate Limit and Fees) Regulations 2004, defines the 'appropriate limit' for the Norfolk Constabulary as £450, and specifies that this sum equates to 18 hours work at a standard rate of £25 per hour. In accordance with Section 17 of the Freedom of Information Act (2000), this serves as a Refusal Notice for your request.

Advice & assistance
The Act requires that the public authority provides advice and assistance to the applicant if it has been refused on the basis of exceeding the appropriate costs limit.

In relation to points 1 and 2 of your request, due to the number of files that would need to be reviewed, it is not possible to advise on refining these questions to bring it within the cost limit. If you were to refine the dates on point 3 of your request to 2009 onwards, we may be able to provide you with the requested data, as we believe this would bring it within the 18 hour limit.

This response will be published on the Norfolk Constabulary's web-site www.norfolk.police.uk under the Freedom of Information pages at Publication Scheme - Disclosure Logs.

Appendix 5

Metropolitan Police

16th May 2014

FOI Request,
Reference No: 2014040000791

I write in connection with your request for information which was received by the Metropolitan Police Service (MPS) on 08/04/2014.

I note you seek access to the following information:-

Please could you provide me with the following information; relating to each year between 2008-2013:-

1. How many police officers were referred for Psychological assessment?

2. How many police officers were diagnosed with PTSD or Psychological injury?

3. How many police officers took early ill health retirement due to PTSD or Psychological injury?

This letter is to inform you that unfortunately it will not be possible to respond to your request within the cost threshold. I hope the following explanation will clarify why it will not be possible to respond to your request within the 18 hour cost threshold stipulated by the FoIA.

In order to assess whether the information that you have requested was held and could be located, retrieved and extracted within the cost limit, I have made some initial enquiries and would advise it would exceed 18 hours to locate and extract the information.

In regards to questions 1 and 2, officers are referred to Occupational Health (OH) by line managers but information by medical condition is not captured in a reportable format. From recent enquiries I can advise you there were roughly 30,000 referrals between 2008 to 2013.

Therefore, in order to locate and extract the information would require a member of police staff to manually search each record in order to answer your specific request. Whilst I am unable to provide you with an exact estimation it is clear this part of your request will exceed the 18 hours threshold under FoIA.

In regard to question 3 OH does not capture the medical condition in a reportable format for those granted ill health retirement. Therefore, in order to locate and extract the information would require a member of police staff to manually search through each ill health retirement file for the same period. I have been informed that there were roughly 350. Once again, it is clear that this in conjunction with question 1 & 2 would exceed the 18 hours threshold under FoIA. In accordance with the Freedom of Information Act 2000, this letter acts as a Refusal Notice.

Appendix 6

Scottish Police Authority
FREEDOM OF INFORMATION (SCOTLAND) ACT 2002, SUBJECT: Police Officers Medically Retired

This FOI request came from another source. This was forwarded on to me in the hope it would answer my request for information (on a similar topic).

I refer to your letter dated 23 December 2013 which was received on 6 January 2014 regarding the above which has been handled in accordance with the Freedom of Information (Scotland) Act 2002 (FOISA).

How many Police Officers (not civilian support staff) has your Force formally medically retired with <u>diagnosed</u> PTSD in the last three years? I believe it may be difficult for you to have 2013 figures to hand and so I would be satisfied with combined figures from 2010, 2011 and 2012.

Your request for information has now been considered and I can advise you that the Police Service of Scotland does not hold all of the information requested by you. In terms of Section 17 of the Act, this letter represents a formal notice that information is not held.

As you may be are aware, as of 1 April 2013, the Police Service of Scotland (PSoS) came into existence which merged all 8 of the former Forces in Scotland. At present not all recording systems have been linked, accordingly, information has to be gathered from each of the former Force areas. Furthermore, not all of the legacy areas used the same recording systems; therefore, the level of information recorded and that can be extracted differs greatly and in most instances is not held.

In this instance, I would advise that contact should be made with the Scottish Police Authority (formerly Scottish Police Services Authority), the non-departmental public body who provided expert policing and support services to Scotland's eight former police forces including the area of business for which you seek information. If you wish to request information from the SPA they can be contacted at the address listed below:

Appendix 7

Barnet, Enfield and Haringey, Mental Health Trust

22nd May 2014

Your application under the Freedom of Information Act for information regarding police officer referrals to mental health services

I am writing in respect of your recent enquiry to the Communications team for information held by Barnet, Enfield and Haringey Mental Health Trust under the provisions of the Freedom of Information Act 2000 which was received on 12 May 201.

We have now processed your request:
Please could you tell me how many police officers have been referred to psychology and psychiatry services and the community mental health team for each year between 200☐ and 2013?

Please could you tell me how many police officers have been diagnosed with PTSD for the same period?

Our response is as follows:

Our patient recording system does not hold details on occupations, therefore we do not hold information on how many police officers have been referred to our services. On this occasion we are unable to supply you with the requested information.

Appendix 8

19th May 2014

Greater Manchester West, Mental Health NHS Foundation Trust

RE: FREEDOM OF INFORMATION ACT 2000 – INFORMATION REQUEST - REF: D4395

Please find our Trust's response in relation to your request for information under the Freedom of Information Act.

Please could you tell me how many police officers have been referred to psychology and psychiatry services and the community mental health team for each year between 2008 and 2013?

Please could you tell me how many police officers have been diagnosed with PTSD for the same period?

The information that you have requested is not held by Greater Manchester West Mental Health NHS Foundation Trust. In order to obtain this information you will need to contact the Freedom of Information Officer for each individual police force.

Appendix 9

14th May 2014

West Midlands Police

FOI Request Reference:

Your request for information, received 29 March 2014 has now been considered and I apologise for the late delivery of this response.

REQUEST/ RESPONSE

Please could you provide me with the following information; relating to each year between 2008-2013:-

How many police officers were referred for Psychological assessment? There is no recorded information held

How many police officers were diagnosed with PTSD or Psychological injury?

2008/09 = 0, 2009/10 = 0, 2010/11 = 0, 2011/12 = 0
2012/13 = 3, 2013/14 = 4

How many police officers took Early ill health retirement due to PTSD or Psychological injury?

= 7

As recommended as good practice by the Information Commissioner's Office a version of this response may be published on the West Midlands Police website.

Bibliography

(2014). Retrieved from Scottish Police Federation: www.spf.org.uk

Accommodation And Compliance Series: Employees With Post Traumatic Stress Disorder. (n.d.). Retrieved 2014, from Job Accomodation Network: http://askjan.org

ACPO. (2012). *Police Health and Safety Guidelines: A Management Benchmarking Standard.* Association of Chief Police Officers.

Annual Leave Policy and Guidance. (2013). Retrieved 2014, from Gwent Police: http://corporate.gwent.police.uk

Atherton, S. (2012). Cops And Bloggers: Exploring The Presence Of Police Culture On The Web. *Internet Journal of Criminology*.

Bakker, A., & Heuven, E. (2006). Emotional Dissonance, Burnout and In-Role Performance Among Nurses and Police Officers. (A. P. Association, Ed.) *International Journal of Stress Management, 13*(4), 423-440.

Carlier, I., Lamberts, R., & Gersons, B. (1997). *Risk Factors for Posttraumatic Stress Symptomatology in Police Officers: A Prospective Analysis (Abstract)*. Retrieved 2014, from The

Journal of Nervous and Mental Disease: http://journals.lww.com

Chan, J. (1997). *Changing Police Culture: Policing In A Multicultural Society.* Cambridge: Cambridge University Press.

(2014). *Code of Ethics.* Coventry: College of Policing.

Coombe, H. (2013). *To What Extent Does Police Occupational Culture Impact On The Social and Domestic Lives Of Police Officers.* Plymouth Law and Criminal Justice Review.

Critical Incident Debrief 'cldB' Force Policy. (2004). Retrieved 2013, from West Mercia Police: www.westmercia.police.uk

Disability discrimination - legal briefing. (n.d.). Retrieved July 2014, from Mind: www.mind.org.uk

Dobby, J., Anscombe, J., & Tuffin, R. (2004). *Police leadership: expectations and impact.* Retrieved 2014, from Internet Memory Foundation: http://collection.europarchive.org

DSM-5 Criteria for PTSD. (2013). Retrieved 2014, from U.S Department Of Veterans Affairs: National Center for PTSD: www.ptsd.va.gov

Early Conciliation. (n.d.). Retrieved July 2014, from ACAS: www.acas.org.uk

(2011). *Employment Statutory Code of Practice.* Equality and Human Rights Commission.

(2014). *Employment Tribunal.* Atom Content Marketing Ltd.

Employment Tribunal Hearings. (n.d.). Retrieved 2014, from Citizens Advice Bureau: www.adviceguide.org.uk

Equality Act 2010 Guidance; Guidance On Matters To Be Taken Into Account In Determining Questions Relating To The Definition Of Disability. (2011, May). Retrieved 2013, from GOV.UK: www.gov.uk

Essex. (2013, May 1st). *PROCEDURE – Police Officers Working Time Regulations.* Retrieved 2014, from Essex Police: www.essex.police.uk

Federation, P. (2009). Retrieved 2014, from British Transport Police Federation: www.btpolfed.org.uk/ref/stressptsd.pdf

Graef, R. (1990). *Talking Blues: The Police In Their Own Words.* London: Fontana Paperbacks.

Hamilton, J. (n.d.). *Work Related Stress and What The Law Says.* Leeds Metropolitan University, Safety, Health and Wellbeing. London: Chartered Institute of Personnel and Development (CIPD).

Hayday, S., Broughton, A., & Tyers, C. (2007). *Managing Sickness Absence In The Police Service: A Review Of Current Practices.* Institute Of Employment Studies. HSE Books.

Herman, J. (1997). *Trauma And Recovery: The Aftermath Of Violence - From Domestic Abuse To Political Terror.* New York: Basic Books.

Hestor, M. (2009). *Who Does What To Whom: Gender and Domestic Violencxe Perpetrators.* Research paper, Bristol University, Violence Against Women Research Group: School for Policy Studies.

Home Office. (2014). *Statistical News Release, Police workforce England and Wales, 30th September 2013.*

House, R. (2013). Life As A Cop: The Impacts of Policing On Police Officers: Is Policing A Lifestyle Choice? (N. T. University, Ed.) *Internet Journal of Criminology.*

Jennings, A. (1994). *On being invisible in the mental health system.* Retrieved 2014, from Sidran: www.sidran.org

Jones, T., Newburn, T., & Smith.D. (1994). *Democracy and Policing.* Policy Studies Institute. London: Policy Studies Institute.

Jung, C. (1995). *Memories, Dreams, Reflections.* London: Fontana Press.

Karpman, S. (1984). Frustration and Burnout. *Eric Berne Seminar*, *4*, pp. 7-11.

Lansing, K. (2012). *The Rite Of Return: Coming Back From Duty-Induced PTSD.* U.S.A: High Ground Press.

Lewis, T. (2008). *Identifying Discrimination in Employment: A Diagnostic and Referral Guide For Busy Advisors.* A Central London Law Center Publication.

Lewis, T. (2011). *Proving Disability and Reasonable Adjustments - A Workers Guide To Evidence Under The Equality Act 2010, Edition 4.* Retrieved 2013, from Equality and Human Rights Commission: www.equalityhumanrights.com

Loftus, B. (2012). *Police Culture In A Changing World.* Oxford: Oxford University Press.

Maguen, S., Metzier, T. M., Inslicht, S., Henn-Haase, C., Neylan, T., & Marmar, C. (2009). Routine Work Environment Stress and PTSD Symptoms in Police Officers. *Journal of Nervous and Mental Disease, 197*(10), 754-760.

Maguire, T. V. (1995-97). *A recovery bill of rights for trauma survivors.* Retrieved 2014, from Sidran:

www.sidran.org

Management Of Stress At Work Policy. (2007). Retrieved 2013, from West Mercia Police: www.westmercia.police.uk

Managing Diversity; Dignity and Respect At Work. (n.d.). Retrieved 2013, from West Mercia Police: www.westmercia.police.uk

Managing Sickness Absence Procedure. (2007). Retrieved 2013, from West Mercia Police: www.westmercia.police.uk

Marmar, C., & McCaslin. (2006). Predictors Of Post-Traumatic Stress In Police And Other First Responders. *Annals New York Academy of Sciences*, 1-18.

Met Police Has 'Culture Of Fear', Officers Say. (2014, April 4th). Retrieved 2014, from BBC News: www.bbc.co.uk

Metcalfe, B., & Dick, G. (2000). Is The Force Still With You? Measuring Police Commitment. *Journal of Managerial Psychology, 15*(8), 812-832.

Mitchell, M., Stevenson, K., & Poole, D. (2001). *Managing Post Incident Reactions In The Police Service.* Sudbury, Suffolk: HSE Books.

Myhill, A., & Quinton, P. (2011). *It's a fair cop? Police*

legitimacy, public co-operation and crime reduction, an interpretive evidence commentary. NPIA (National Policing Improvement Agency).

National Collaborating Centre for Mental Health Royal College of Psychiatrists', R. U. (2005). *NICE Guidelines: Post Traumatic Stress Disorder: The management of PTSD in adults and children in primary and secondary care.* National Institution Clinical Excellence. Gaskell and the British Psychological Society.

Norman, S., Elbogen, E., & Schnurr, P. (2014). *Research Findings on PtSD and Violence*. Retrieved 2014, from U.S Department of Veterans Affairs, National Center for PTSD: www.ptsd.va.gov

Oliver, W., & Meier, C. (2009). Considering The Efficacy Of Stress Management Education On Small-Town And Rural Police. *Applied Psychology in Criminal Justice, 5*(1).

Paws for Purple Hearts. (n.d.). Retrieved 2014, from www.pawsforpurplehearts.org

Police Federation backs new ethics code for officers. (n.d.). Retrieved 07 14, 2014, from BBC News: www.bbc.co.uk/news/uk-28277417

(2012). *Police Officer Misconduct, Unsatisfactory Performance and Attendance Management*

Procedures. Guidance, Home Office.

(2010). *Police Pension Scheme Injury Award Procedure: Injury Award Procedure, Version 9.* Cambridgeshire Constabulary.

Police Service Strength. (2013, July). Retrieved 2014, from Parliament UK: www.parliament.uk

Policing by Consent. (n.d.). Retrieved 2014, from Gov.UK: www.gov.uk

Price, J. (2014). *When a child's parent has PTSD.* Retrieved 2014, from U.S Department of Veterans Affairs, National Center for PTSD: www.ptsd.va.gov

Psychological Assistance Dogs UK (PAD). (n.d.). Retrieved July 2014, from www.padogsuk.org

Regel, S., & Joseph, S. (2010). *Post-traumatic Stress: the facts.* New York: Oxford University Press.

Salston, M., & Figley, C. (2003). *Secondary Traumatic Stress Effects of Working With Survivors of Criminal Victimization.* Journal of Traumatic Stress.

Shay, J. (2002). *Odysseus In America: Combat Trauma And The Trials Of Homecoming.* New York, U.S.A: Scribner.

Shay, J. (2003). *Achilles In Vietnam: Combat Trauma And The Undoing Of Character* (First ed.). New York, U.S.A: Scribner.

Skolnick, J. (1966). *Justice Without Trial: Law Enforcement In Democratic Society.* U.S.A: John Wiley & Sons, Inc.

Sommers, J. (2013). *Quarter Of Officers At High PTSD Risk*. Retrieved 2014, from Police Oracle: www.policeoracle.com

The Scottish Government. (2014). *Police Officer Quarterly Strength Statistics Scotland.*

The Workplace Wellbeing Charter: Self-Assessment Standards. (n.d.). Retrieved 2014, from www.wellbeingcharter.org.uk

Trochim, W. (2006). *Statistical Terms in Sampling*. Retrieved 2014, from Research Methods Knowledge Base: www.socialresearchmethods.net

Wagner, S. (n.d.). The "Rescue Personality": Fact or Fiction? *The Australasian Journal of Disaster and Trauma Studies, 2005-2.*

USEFUL LINKS

National Association of Retired Police Officers (NARPO)
38, Bond St
Wakefield
West Yorkshire
WF1 2QP
Tel: 01924 362166
Email : hq@narpo.org

Police Dependants' Trust
3 Mount Mews,
High Street,
Hampton,
Middlesex,
TW12 2SH
Telephone: 020 8941 6907
E-mail: office@pdtrust.org

Every year hundreds of police officers suffer serious injuries on duty. Sadly, some of these officers lose their lives. We provide financial support to help ease some of the pressures police families face when an officer has been killed or injured on duty.

COPS
Care Of Police Survivors (COPS),
PO Box 5685,
Rugeley,
WS15 9DN
Telephone
0844 893 2055
admin@ukcops.org
www.ukcops.org

COPS is a UK registered charity helping families of police officers who have lost their lives on duty, rebuild their lives.

The Gurney Fund for Police Orphans
9 Bath Road
Worthing BN11 3NU
Tel: 01903 237256

The Fund may help children not only of Police Officers who have died, but of those who have taken early retirement on ill-health grounds within the 22 subscribing Forces.

Safe Horizon UK
Independent advocacy and support service for Police Officers and their families, affected by psychological injury, mental ill health and occupational stress.

www.safehorizon.co.uk
safehorizonuk@orange.net

Anxiety UK
Zion Community Resource Centre
339 Stretford Road,
Hulme,
Manchester M15 4ZY
Helpline: 08444 775 774
www.anxietyuk.org.uk

Anxiety UK works to relieve and support those living with anxiety disorders by providing information, support and understanding via an extensive range of services.

Mind Infoline (Information and Support)
PO Box 277
Manchester
M60 3XN
0300 123 3393
info@mind.org.uk
Text: 86463

Mind LAS (Legal Advice Line)
PO Box 277
Manchester
M60 3XN
0300 466 6463
legal@mind.org.uk
www.mind.org.uk

PAD (Psychological Assistance Dogs UK)
Non-Profit Organisation providing those with psychological disability with a trained assistance dog with legal access to premises (as with Guide Dogs for the Blind)
www.padogsuk.org

ABOUT THE AUTHOR

I have worked in Domestic Abuse services for 10 years; at women's refuge, safe house accommodation and outreach support in the community.

I worked as an IDVA (Independent Domestic Violence Advocate) with high risk cases, attending court to provide support and working with clients to create a personal safety plan. I acquired my Diploma in Hypnotherapy and NLP (Neuro Linguistic Programming) and completed training in Programme delivery for victims of Domestic Abuse.

I then went on to provide front line management to Ex-offender services and Domestic Abuse Services simultaneously.

I secured a management position with a Voluntary Male Perpetrator Programme (a strengths based model) and completed training in Motivational Interviewing and Perpetrator programme facilitation.

I implemented the programme into Support services and had responsibility for the overall management of the service; including creating local policies and procedures, supervision of programme delivery, case management, ensuring good practice and line management. Prior to Domestic Abuse, I worked in Home Care as an Assistant Manager and healthcare assistant.

My husband suffered a stress breakdown and was diagnosed with PTSD. I spent the following 20 months as carer and advocate, managing his communications with his employer, keeping records, dealing with legal action and pursuing his entitlements (in terms of dignity, respect and employment rights). Our experiences were the inspiration for this book and Safe Horizon UK.

I began Safe Horizon UK to help and support other Officers and families because we felt this service was greatly needed. We would have valued support, guidance and community during our own experience. Instead, we were isolated and had to carry out our own extensive research in order to understand PTSD, my husbands' rights and organizational systems, policies and procedures. Safe Horizon UK aims to utilize this information to serve others and provide a signposting, advocacy and advice service.

You are invited to review 'Duty of Care' and send your comments via www.safehorizon.co.uk or direct to safehorizonuk@orange.net

A

ACPO, 91, *See* Leadership
Anger, 26, 133, 143, 144, *See* HSE - Health & Safety Executive

B

Behaviour, 12, 133, 163
Brain functioning, 25
Burnout, 19, 35, 38, 40, 44, 54, 166

C

Chan, J, 32, 44, 47, 56, 74
Children, 144, 158, 160, 161, 162
Civilian support staff, 70
    Deviancy. *See* Police Culture: Deviancy
    Power and Control. *See* Police Culture: Power and Control
Civilian values. *See* Police Culture: Community Policing
Code of Ethics, 22, 23, 33, 78, 80, 81, 88, 92, 93, 119
Cognitive Dissonance, 41, *See* Police Culture: Antagonism
Compassion Fatigue, 16, 27, 48, 155, 156, 157, 166
Complex PTSD, 19
Criminal offence, 133, 147

D

Data collection, 63
Dealing with trauma, 20, 129, 130
Diagnosis, 150, 151, 152
Disability, 88, 96, 97, 113, 122, 123, 135, 150-152
Discrimination, 113, 152, 154
Domestic Violence, 145, 156, 158, 162, 163
DSM-5 criteria, 10

E

Education, 83, 94, 100
Emotional Dissonance, 53
Emotional symptoms, 12

F

Financial impact, 67, 72, 114, 115, 116, 135, 173, 174

G

Graef, R, 29, 32, 41, 53, 74

H

Herman, J, 16, 29, 39, 54, 61, 105
HSE - Health & Safety Executive, 18, 60, 79, 99, *See* Research

J

Justice, 21

K

Karpman, 51
    Drama triangle, 38, 39, 51, 54

L

Lansing, K, 25, 26, 43
Leadership, 21, 23, 34, 43, 54, 57, 77, *See* Organizational factors
Loftus, B, 31, 33, 36, 40, 42, 48, 52, 55, 56, 74

M

Moral character, 26, 136, 138, 166

O

Occupational stress, 58
Officer led support, 82, 84, 96, 97, 100, 102, 105, 108, 117, 119-122
Organizational factors, 35, 40, 43- 45, 50, 54, 56, 71, 75, 77-80, 82, 84, 118, 165, 166, 167, *See* Anger, *See* Leadership, *See* Police Culture: Disciplinary
Organizational support, 35, 44, 59, 60, 82, 94, 95, 97, 98, 101, 120, 166, 167, 168, *See* Leadership, *See* Psychological Injury: Prevention

P

Personal Trauma, 20
Physical evidence of Injury, 25
Physiological symptoms, 11, 132, 133
Police Culture, 48, 55, 56, 164, 166
    Abuse, 17, 32, 48, 78, 81, *See* Organizational factors
    Antagonism, 40
    Barriers to identifying PTSD, 14
    Captivity, 41, 50, 83, 84, 91
    Community Policing, 32, 33, 37, 43, 60, 88, *See* Graef, R
    Comradery, 32
    Deviancy, 49, 72, 90-92, 106, 109, 127
    Disciplinary, 32, 33, 45
    Diversity, 17, 31, 32
    Humour, 42
    Loss of individuality, 17
    National Policing pride, 75
    Openness, 19, 109
    Organizational factors, 91
    Political Correctness, 31
    Power and Control, 49, 89, *See* Captivity
    Sense of mission, 34, 36, 54
    Stress, 18
    Symbolic Assailant, 34
Police Personality, 33, 34, 36, 40, 50, 52
Police reform, 46, 56
Psychological Injury, 9
    Affects on daily living, 23, 105, 133-135, 137, 139, 145
    Causes of, 18, 21, 27, 57, *See* Organizational factors,
    Complex PTSD, 58, 133
    Diagnostic criteria, 10

Flashbacks, 10, 28
Hallucination, 27, 29
Hypervigilance, 34
Intrusive memories, 28
Isolation, 26, 143
Maladaptive behaviour, 25, 40, 57
Perception, 27, 53, 100
Prevention, 23, 73, 118, 167, 168, 170
Reasonable adjustment, 108, 111, 121, 123, 124
Recovery, 82, 84, 130, 136-139, 142, 143
Revenge, 27
Single traumatic event, 20, 99, 166
Threat, 27
Psychological symptoms, 12, 132, 133
Psychology assessment, 124

R

Recovery, 22
Relationship, 156, 157
Rescuer, 38, 39, 51
Research, 35, 57, 66, 70, 79, 99
Resolution, 22
Risk assessment, 148
Risk of harm, 80, 93, 133, 143, 145, 158, *See* Domestic Violence

S

Secondary Traumatic Stress (STS), 16, 27, 76, 166
Sense of mission, 51-52
Shay, J, 19, 53, 75
   Maladaptive behaviour, 25
   Moral Injury, 19, 21
Skolnick J. *See* Cognitive Dissonance
   Symbolic Assailant, 34
Suicide, 146-147, 159
Support network, 138-145, 164

T

Traumatic Countertransference, 39
Traumatic events on duty, 15

V

Vicarious Traumatization (VT), 27